Managing for a Change

How to run community development projects

ANTHONY DAVIES

ITDG
PUBLISHING

Published by ITDG Publishing
103–105 Southampton Row, London WC1B 4HL, UK
www.itdgpublishing.org.uk

First published in 1997
Reprinted 2000, 2001

ISBN 1 85339 399 1

A catalogue record for this book is available from the British Library.

ITDG Publishing is the publishing arm of the Intermediate Technology Development Group.
Our mission is to build the skills and capacity of people in developing countries through the
dissemination of information in all forms, enabling them to improve the quality of their lives and
that of future generations.

VSO, 317 Putney Bridge Road, London SW15 2PN, UK. Website: www.vso.org.uk Reg. UK charity
no 313757

VSO is an international development agency working through volunteers to tackle disadvantage and
realise people's potential. VSO Books publishes practical books and Working Papers in education and
development based on current thinking and the professional experience of VSO volunteers and their
overseas partners.

Typeset by J&L Composition Ltd, Filey, North Yorkshire
Printed in UK by SRP, Exeter

Contents

Acknowledgements

The making of this book spans many years, during which time I have had the privilege of working with dedicated project managers, community groups and individuals; there are too many people to name individually, but I am grateful to them all.

A special thanks must be given to my ex-colleagues working for British Petroleum Development Limited, for giving me an insight into the professional management of projects. Also to the artisans and traders of Suame Magazine, Kumasi, Ghana, an example of self-help and perseverance in the face of adversity, *madase paa*. Special thanks to the Amerindian communities of the Essequibo Coast, Guyana, for the insight into achieving sustainable solutions to problems through community self realization. I am grateful to both the Ashanti and Amerindian communities I have worked with for their good humour and hospitality, which will remain a treasured memory.

Two organizations made the publication of this book possible:

- The Inter-American Institute for Cooperation on Agriculture. It was a true joy and pleasure to work with the IICA staff in Guyana. Words are inadequate to register my gratitude for their material assistance, advice and encouragement.
- Voluntary Service Overseas, who made it possible for me to work as a VSO volunteer in Ghana and Guyana, and also as a UNV in Guyana. This book is largely based on that VSO experience of working with community groups. Sincere gratitude for providing a grant from the VSO Central Project Fund which enabled the original publication of the book in Guyana.

My gratitude for assistance in finalizing the draft of the first edition goes to Bonita Harris for her review and suggestions and to Atma Shivbarran for preparing the layout.

I am also indebted to the Guyana Book Foundation, who sponsored the printing of additional copies of the first edition for distribution to schools and libraries in Guyana.

This book is dedicated to all those members of community development groups who, despite receiving little thanks or acknowledgement, dedicate their time and efforts to undertaking community development projects. Theirs is the true achievement.

Ma, diolch am pob peth.

A many-storeyed tower is built by placing one brick upon another.

TAO TE CHING, by Lao Tzu.

Introduction

Eight out of every ten development projects fail! Why? Is it so difficult to plan and manage a project successfully? Or were the groups who undertook the projects ill prepared? The answer is partly both. Project management is a profession; like farming or food preparation, it is a skill we have to learn. Too often, community groups rely only on good intentions and enthusiasm to guide them along the path of project planning and implementation.

It is not possible, in a book this size, to cover in great detail all the specialist skills and techniques required for project management. Indeed, the subjects covered in each chapter here deserve a book in their own right.

This book will provide community groups with an insight into development project planning and management. It will also give step-by-step guidance through the stages from project identification to post-project activities.

The book is organized into nine chapters, set out in the same order as the stages required when managing a project:

Chapter 1
PROBLEM IDENTIFICATION
Projects often fail because they attempt to solve the wrong problem. The first stage in any project is to identify the core problems and their causes. Not all the members of a community will be supportive of a project. It is important to identify those who will be interested in giving assistance and those who could obstruct the progress of the project.

Chapter 2
MOBILIZING A GROUP
The more people involved with a project the better the chance of it succeeding and obtaining assistance from external agencies. The group members will have to organize their activities. A committee will have to be elected and its members trained to perform their duties efficiently. Meetings will have to be held and decisions taken. All the group members will have to take an active part.

Chapter 3
SOLUTION IDENTIFICATION AND PLANNING
Once the group has organized itself, the members should agree on the problem(s) to be solved. Thought should also be given to obtaining training for the members. The next stage is to set objectives for the project – what the group members hope to achieve. Consideration must be given to 'sustainability': the ability of the project to continue to provide a solution to the problem for as long as is required. The actions required to achieve the objectives must be identified and planned. Planning plays a key part in ensuring that the project is success-fully managed.

Chapter 4
RESOURCE IDENTIFICATION AND COST ESTIMATING
With activities agreed upon by the group members and a project plan prepared, the resource

requirements must be identified. What skills do the group members have? How much will the project cost? When will the funds be required?

Chapter 5
PROJECT FUNDING

A decision will have to be made on how to finance the project. Has the group sufficient resources or will it have to seek assistance from external organizations? What type of funding will be sought: a loan or a grant? Who can provide loans and grants? How does a group apply for a loan or a grant? How can contact be made with funding agencies?

Chapter 6
BASIC BOOKKEEPING AND RECORDS

Most projects will require the spending of money. It might be funds provided by the group members or from an external organization. Whatever the case, records will have to be kept of every transaction. This will require the keeping of accounts. Accounts by themselves are not sufficient; proof of expenditure must also be provided, with receipts, bills and other records kept. Things can go wrong if only the group's treasurer understands the accounts; all committee members should know and understand the procedures used. It is likely that the group will have to open a bank account. How is this done? What type of account should the group have?

Chapter 7
PROJECT SUPERVISION

During the project the group will have to use management skills. These will include using the project plan and budget to determine whether the project is proceeding as desired. Good managers do not allow things just to happen, they look forward and predict what might happen. Then they control events to achieve the desired objectives. The success of the project will depend upon the group members cooperating and working together. Even in harmonious groups, misunderstandings can arise. Group leaders must be skilled in getting the members to work as a team, assisting and supporting one another. Decisions, and when necessary corrective actions, will have to be taken when things go wrong.

Chapter 8
PROJECT EXECUTION

With the group trained in the necessary management skills, and the resources available, the group can begin the project. Material and equipment might have to be purchased. Activities will have to be organized. Labour must be arranged. The progress of the project will have to be measured and events controlled. The group committee will have to provide reports to the members and, if external funding was obtained, to donor agencies, giving details of events and proof of all expenditure.

Chapter 9
POST-PROJECT ACTIVITIES

What happens when the group has achieved its planned project objectives? If it is successful the members can justifiably be proud of their efforts and congratulate each other. But first there are some administrative matters to deal with. The project 'books' have to be 'closed', that is, the final financial accounts have to be prepared and audited. This is necessary to check that all the money received by the group can be accounted for.

When can a project be considered to be finished? The answer is when its results cease to serve a useful purpose. The Egyptian pyramids were built in Africa thousands of years ago, as tombs for their kings. Yet today they still serve a useful purpose as a tourist attraction and so have to be maintained and managed. So it is with most projects; they will only continue to serve the needs of the community if they are managed and looked after. Who will continue to manage the operation of the project? Will it be the same committee or should a new management committee be chosen? What are the management skills that will be required? Will additional training be required? Will funds be required for the ongoing operation? Like the successful management of the project, the future success of the operation will depend upon good management, planning and budgeting.

The book describes in simple terms the stages and procedures that can be followed by a group to manage a community development project successfully. It is not a textbook, but a guide to assist a group to make its own decisions on managing its project. The types of community projects are so varied that it is not possible to give examples to cover all eventualities. The examples are therefore used to illustrate general ideas.

The questions and exercises at the end of each chapter do not comprise a list of all the steps a group has to take in order to manage a community development project successfully. Projects are so varied that each one must be planned and managed to meet its individual requirements, and the questions are designed to assist you to manage your own project. No answers are provided, only questions! However, they have been devised so that you ask and answer them at the appropriate time. These sections are not included to test or trap you; they are provided to assist you by suggesting questions that should be considered when a group manages a community development project.

CHAPTER 1
Problem identification

Which comes first? Choosing a project, or forming a community development group? The answer is neither. If the project comes first, it is like an answer looking for a question! If a development group is formed first, it is like a group looking for something to do in order to justify its existence. If it is not the project or the group that comes first, then what does come first?

> It's the
> **problem**
> that comes first

If you do not have a problem, then you do not need a project. Projects are undertaken in order to solve a problem. It is a foolish person who goes looking for a problem! Life is such that problems come looking for you!

So you think that you have a problem. What exactly is it? Think before you answer, because it might not be the problem you think you have. Too often, projects fail because groups jump in too soon with an inappropriate solution, just because they did not spend a little time to understand fully the situation and to identify the true problem.

> The secret of solving a problem is
> proper problem identification

Cause–effect relationship

A problem does not happen in isolation. It has a cause and it will have an effect.

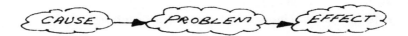

1

Example

For some years the mains water supply pipeline has been out of service. So households have to rely on storing rain water. It is now the dry season. Last week, the last of the water was used from the storage tank.

Cause	–	*The storage tank is empty.*
Problem	–	*There is no water in the house.*
Effect	–	*There is no water for washing.*

In this example, there would appear to be a simple problem to identify. But notice, the effect also becomes a problem, so the original problem has become a cause. And a chain is set up of Cause → Problem → Effect:

Example

In the above example, the new problem, There is no water for washing, *can in turn become a cause, leading to yet another problem:*

New cause	–	*There is no water for washing.*
New problem	–	*Nothing can be washed.*
New effect	–	*The household is not as clean as it should be.*

In the above analysis it was assumed that the problem arose because of one original cause. But in most cases, problems result from more than one cause.

Example

In the above example, the original problem was: There is no water in the house. *And the original cause identified was:* The storage tank is empty. *But another cause is that:* The mains water supply is not working:

Cause	–	*The storage tank is empty.*
Cause	–	*The mains water supply is out of order.*
Problem	–	*We have no water in the house.*
Effect	–	*There is no water for washing.*

Just as a problem can be the result of more than one cause, one problem can have more than one effect.

Example

The original problem was: There is no water in the house. *And the original effect:* There is no water for washing. *But another effect could be:* There is no water to water the garden.

Cause	–	The storage tank is empty.
Problem	–	We have no water in the house.
Effect	–	There is no water to water the garden.
Effect	–	There is no water for washing.

It can therefore be seen that even for a simple problem there are many combinations of causes, problems and effects. So the causes, problems and effects form a complicated network stretching in all directions.

If the relationships are so intricate, how will it ever be possible to identify the 'true' problem?

Simple, just take it one step at a time.

Problem analysis

There are many ways to identify the 'true' or **core problem**. Two such methods are:

- The use of the 'problem tree' method
  and
- The use of a 'problem analysis' chart.

PROBLEM TREE METHOD

The problem tree[1] method is simply a way of drawing out the cause and effect relationship regarding a particular problem situation. In drawing your problem tree, locate the causes at lower levels and the effects at the upper levels. The **core problem** connects the two. Thus, the tree trunk represents the core problem, the roots are the causes, and the branches represent the effects. The more basic the causes, the more likely they are to lie at the lower levels of the diagram. The location of a problem on the tree diagram does not necessarily indicate its level of importance.

There is no single correct way of drawing up a problem tree diagram. Different individuals or groups, given the same list of problems and causes, will normally organize them differently in a tree diagram. This is due to the different levels of knowledge and experience of each person, and the amount of time available for analysis.

To illustrate the use of this method, the example of not having any water supply for the house can be analysed.

Step 1

The group doing the analysis makes a list of the problems together with their causes and effects.

PROBLEM	CAUSE	EFFECT
MAINS WATER SUPPLY IS OUT OF ORDER	BREAK IN MAINS PIPELINE	NO WATER TO WASH
WATER STORAGE TANK EMPTY	NO RAIN FOR THREE MONTHS	NO WATER FOR BATHING AND WASHING CLOTHES
CREEK WATER SALTY	DRY SEASON, FLOW OF WATER FROM THE SEA	NO WATER TO WATER GARDEN

Step 2

Each of the causes and effects are written out on separate cards or pieces of paper.

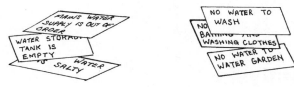

---

[1] A full description of this method can be found in *Commodity Systems Assessment Methodology for Problem and Project Identification*, by Jerry La Gra, IICA 1990.

Step 3

The group discusses the relationship between the causes and the effects. Then, using sticky tape to fix them, the cards are arranged on a wall in the form of the problem tree. Place the causes where the roots would be and the effects where the branches would be. Start by placing the most basic causes at the lowest level, then work your way up.

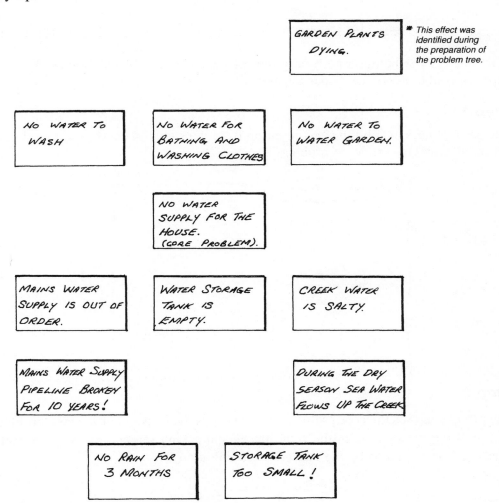

PROBLEM ANALYSIS CHART

Again, the example of not having any water supply for the house is used to illustrate this analysis method.

A problem analysis chart can be used. It is divided into four or more columns, as follows (sub-divide columns for a more complicated analysis):

(4) Root Cause(s)	(3) Cause(s)	(2) Core Problem	(1) Effect(s)

If the analysis is being done by a group of people, use a blackboard or flip-chart paper to enable everyone to participate fully.

Step 1

The group enters in column (2) – counting from the right – what they consider to be the main problem, the 'core problem'.

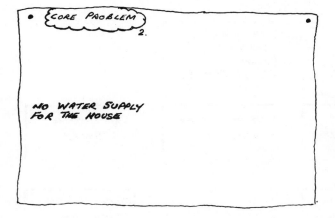

Step 2

The group analyses the core problem and identifies the cause(s) of the core problem. This will require looking in the right places and asking searching questions. Enter what are considered to be the cause(s) into column (3).

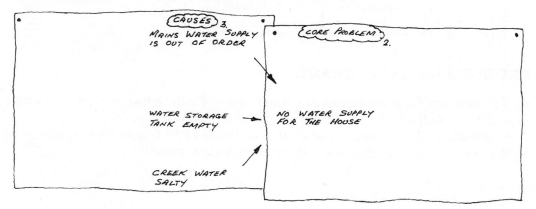

Step 3

The group examines the cause(s) and decides whether these are the 'root cause(s)' or if there are more important or initial causes to the problem. Enter these into column (4).

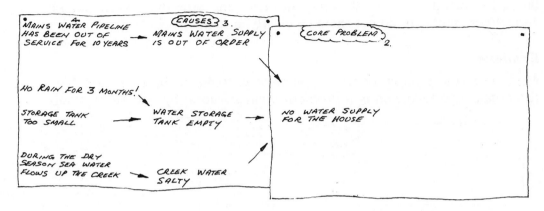

Step 4

The group must now determine whether the initial identification of the core problem was correct. Identify the effect(s) of the core problem and write these in column (1). These are again examined so that the group can decide whether any represents a bigger problem than the initial core problem. If not, it can be assumed that the initial choice was correct. If, however, one of the effects is considered to be a bigger problem, then using a new form or chart, enter the effect as the new core problem and repeat the analysis, steps 1 to 4.

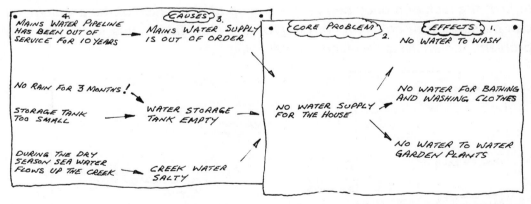

There are three possible sources of water supply to the house, from the mains supply, stored rain water and water collected from a nearby creek. All are independent of each other. It can be seen that the root causes are: the broken mains supply pipeline, that not enough rain water can be collected and during the dry season the creek becomes salty. The root problems to be solved are therefore:

- *The storage tank is too small to store enough water for the dry season.
  and/or*
- *The mains water supply pipeline is not operating.*

The above was a relatively straightforward example where the core problem could be easily identified. The following illustrates the procedure when possibly the correct core problem did not show up clearly at first.

Example

Many farmers' groups identify their main problem to be that their farms are too small. The following is a problem analysis done by one such group.

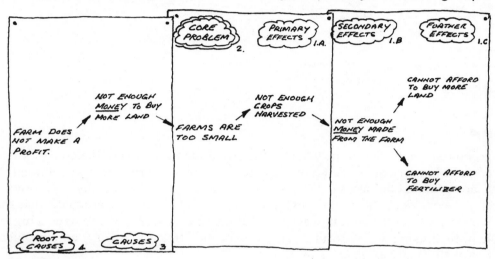

In fact, the lack of money began to show up as the cause of the problem, as can be seen from columns (4), (3), (1b) and (1c). Taking this to be the core problem, the analysis revealed the following:

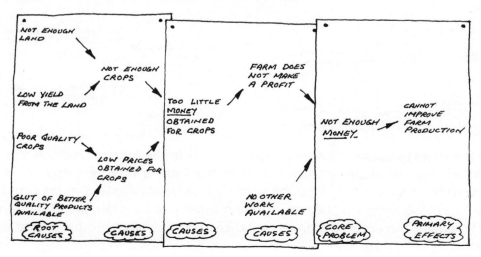

8

Here it can be seen that, in addition to the shortage of land, there are other problems to be considered, including the choice of crop to be grown and the quality of the land. The root problems to be solved are therefore:

- *Insufficient land.*
- *Poor quality land.*
- *Choice of crops to be grown.*

Notice that the number of columns used in the problem analysis can be varied to suit the needs of the analysis. There might be a need to look further back in the chain of causes until the root cause(s) are identified, or to ensure that the correct core problem has been identified to examine the chain of primary and secondary effect(s). In either case the format can be altered to assist with the analysis.

A problem analysis chart can be used to analyse and identify even very complicated situations with a number of either inter-related or independent causes of problems. With the correct use of the procedure the root problems can be identified.

Community analysis

While analysing the problem, it will be seen how the problem affects various members of the community. Some might be negatively affected while others might be benefiting from the current situation. It is likely that those who are disadvantaged would support a project to change the situation. Those who are currently benefiting may oppose any change. In Chapter 2, a description is given of how a group can be formed to manage a project with the objective of solving the identified problem. First, however, the members of the community who will support the project, as well as those who will oppose it, have to be identified.

This can be done with the aid of a community analysis chart. The chart is completed as follows:

Step 1

List all the groups that exist in the community. These could include: church, youth, women, parent-teachers, sports, farmers, craft, political parties, and so on. For each group enter on the form how they are affected positively and negatively by the problem.

COMMUNITY MEMBERS AND GROUPS	HOW AFFECTED ?	
	Positive Effects	Negative Effects
COMMUNITY GROUPS: - - - -		
FAMILIES: - - - -		
INDIVIDUALS: - - -		
ONGOING PROJECTS: - - - -		

Step 2

List all the families in the community. Enter how they are affected positively and negatively.

Step 3

List all the key individuals in the community, including both the formal and informal leaders. Enter how they are affected positively and negatively.

Step 4

There could be projects being planned or already being undertaken in the community. These could be managed by the national government, community or regional council, community groups, private individuals or families. These could be affected by a new project. List the negative or positive effects.

> Find out
> who will support
> and
> who will oppose any project

Example

Applying this procedure to the farmers' group, with the root problems:

- *Insufficient land.*
- *Poor quality land.*
- *Choice of crops to be grown.*

COMMUNITY MEMBERS AND GROUPS	HOW AFFECTED ?	
	Positive Effects	Negative Effects
COMMUNITY GROUPS: - *Community Farm Association* - *Parent-Teachers Group* - -	*No benefits.* *Improved farming would provide more food for the children.*	*Improvements in crops would be additional competition in the market.* *Headmaster and teachers want the land for their own use.*
FAMILIES: - *Williams, Person and Fredericks* - *Rodrigues and Charles* - -	*These families are in the similar position and would support the project.* -	*No negative effects.* *These families are the biggest farmers and want all the additional land for their own use.*
INDIVIDUALS: - *Henry Lewis (Chairman of Village Council)* - *Charles James (Former Headmaster)* - *Marry Lloyd*	*Is also trying to improve the production from his farm.* *Supports all activities that could improve the quality of life of community members.* -	*He will not want to upset the main land owning families just before an election.* - *Buys most of the farm products, to sell in her shop in town. Would oppose any competition*
ONGOING PROJECTS: - *School building* - *Community Boat* - *Women's Farm Group*	*Will not be affected* *If more crops were grown there would be more freight for the boat to carry.* -	- - *If families have bigger farms, the women would not have time to work on the Women's Farm Project.*

The chart shows a small sample of the details that could be recorded. In practice, far more groups and individuals would be identified for detailed analysis.

A project is more likely to succeed if it receives support from a large number of residents. Also, a project benefiting or supported by the majority of the community is more likely to receive assistance from external organizations, including funding agencies. By means of a community analysis, those groups and individuals who will support a project can be identified. The analysis also permits the identification of the reasons why people might oppose the project. This information can be used either:

- To persuade people to change their minds and support the project.
  or
- To design a project that would not meet so much resistance.

> **The more support a project has, the more likely it is to succeed**

If the problem analysis is performed before a group has been formed, the next step will be to organize a group to identify a solution for the problem. After the group has been formed, and before any attempt is made to identify solutions, the problem analysis and community analysis procedures described in this chapter should be repeated. WHY?

The two main reasons are:

- To obtain the support of all the group members, they should be given the opportunity of agreeing on the root problems to be solved.
- When performing a problem analysis, the more people with a variety of relevant experience who participate, the greater the chance of identifying the correct answers. If all the members of the group have the opportunity to take part, more expertise will be available.

> **Community members should be encouraged not only to support, but also to participate in all project activities**

Questions and exercises

The following questions and exercises relate to the subjects covered in this chapter. **They have not been devised as a test** of what you know. They are meant to encourage participants to **understand and analyse the problem fully, before the group chooses a solution**.

    Please read the whole chapter before attempting the exercises and questions. If at any time you are unsure, refer back to the relevant section.

Question: Why is there a risk of the project failing if the solution is selected too soon?

Question: What could happen if the problem is not correctly analysed?

Exercise: *Make a list of people who can assist you in analysing the problem. Then seek their assistance.*

PROBLEM ANALYSIS

Depending on the preferred method, refer to the 'Problem tree' or 'Problem analysis chart' method.

Problem tree method

Exercise: *Make a list of what are considered to be the problems and their causes.*

Question: Have all the causes and effects been identified?

Question: What are the most important problems?

Question: What is the main problem that you have to solve (that is, the 'core problem')?

Exercise: *Write out separate cards or pieces of paper for each cause and each effect giving brief details.*

Exercise: *Arrange the cards in the form of a problem tree with the causes at the lower level, and the effects placed above the core problem.*

Question: Do the participants agree that the correct core problem has been identified?

Question: Do you need to identify a new core problem?

Question: Have all the causes been identified, and are they placed in the correct position on the problem tree?

Question: Have all the effects been identified?

Question: What are the 'root causes' of the problem?

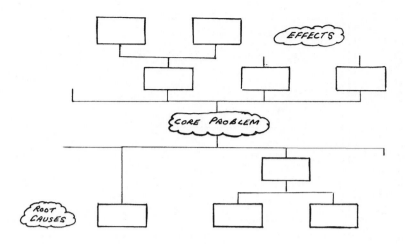

When you are confident that the core problem and root causes have been identified, proceed to the 'Community analysis' section.

Problem analysis chart

Exercise: What is the main problem, that is, the **'core problem'**, you have to solve? Prepare a problem analysis chart and enter the answer in column 2.

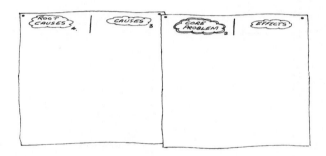

Question: How can you identify the cause(s) of the core problem?

Question: What are the questions that need to be asked when analysing the causes?

Question: What are the cause(s) of the core problem? Are they the only ones?

Exercise: Enter the cause(s) in column 3a of the problem analysis chart.

Question: What is meant by the term 'root cause'?

SAMPLE PROBLEM ANALYSIS CHART

ROOT CAUSES Column 4	CAUSE(S) Column 3c	CAUSE(S) Column 3b	CAUSE(S) Column 3a	CORE PROBLEM Column 2	EFFECT(S) Primary Column 1a	EFFECT(S) Secondary Column 1b

Exercise: *Analyse the causes listed in column 3a, and decide whether all are the root causes of the problem. If they are not, then they are in turn the effects of more important causes. Enter these newly identified causes in column 3b.*

Exercise: *Analyse the causes listed in column 3b, and decide whether these are the root cause of the problem. If they are not the root cause, then they are in turn the effects of more important causes. Enter the newly identified causes in column 3c. **Repeat the analysis until the root cause(s) have been identified.***

Question: How do you test whether the correct core problem has been correctly identified?

Exercise: *Examine the core problems listed in column 2, and decide what will be the effects of these problems. List the answers in column 1a.*

Exercise: *Examine the effects listed in column 1a, and decide whether they in turn will result in a problem. What would the effects of the new problem be? List the answers in column 1b.*

Question: Are the effects listed in columns 1a and 1b a bigger problem than those first identified as the core problem listed in column 2? If they are, what does that mean?

Question: Do you need to identify a new core problem?

Question: What are the root cause(s) of the problem?

Question: If the number of columns in the problem analysis chart is not enough, what can be done?

When you are confident that the core problem and root causes have been identified, proceed to the 'Community analysis' section.

Community analysis

Question: Do projects benefit all members of the community?

Question: Why do some members of a community oppose a project that would benefit large numbers of the community?

Question: Are there people in your community likely to object to a project being undertaken?

Exercise: *Prepare a community analysis form and list all the groups active in the community.*

SAMPLE COMMUNITY ANALYSIS FORM

COMMUNITY MEMBERS AND GROUPS	HOW AFFECTED ?	
	Positive Effects	Negative Effects
COMMUNITY GROUPS: ı ı ı ı ı		
FAMILIES: ı ı ı ı ı		
INDIVIDUALS: ı ı ı ı ı		
ONGOING PROJECTS: ı ı ı ı ı		

Question: Will the members of the groups be positively or negatively affected by the proposed project?

Exercise: *List on the form how they will be affected.*

Question: Who are the main families in the community?

Exercise: *List the names of the families on the form.*

Question: Will the members of these families be positively or negatively affected by the proposed project?

Exercise: *List on the form how they will be affected.*

Question: Who are the people who have influence in the community?

Exercise: *List their names on the form.*

Question: Will these individuals be positively or negatively affected by the proposed project?

Exercise: *List on the form how they will be affected.*

Question: Are there any other projects being planned or undertaken in the community?

Exercise: *List, on the form, the project and the groups managing them.*

Question: Will these projects be positively or negatively affected by the proposed project?

Exercise: *List on the form how they will be affected.*

Encourage people to participate

Exercise: *Examine the form, and identify the main **positive** effects of the proposed project.*

Question: Are there any groups or individuals who might object to the proposed project?

Question: What will be their main objections?

Exercise: *Prepare a list of points that can be used in discussions with groups and individuals who might object to the project. You want to persuade them that the project will be good for the community.*

Question: Is it possible to get the support of all members of the community?

Question: What can be done to gain the support of as many groups and individuals as possible?

Question: Why is it important to get the support of as many groups and individuals as possible?

Question: Did all the members of the group take part in the analysis to identify the 'root problems' to be solved?

Question: Why is it important to give all the members of the group the opportunity to participate in identifying the root problems?

CHAPTER 2
Mobilizing a group

The first step

Having identified the problem, a decision must now be taken about what to do. When problems are too large or complicated for one person or family to solve, assistance can be sought from others who are in similar circumstances.

The first thing to do is to identify people who might be prepared to work together. Discuss with neighbours and friends and get a feeling of what they think about the problem. See whether they are prepared to do something about it. If there is enough interest then a decision can be taken on whether a group should be formed to solve the problem.

At this stage care must be taken not to upset people who see themselves as the leaders of the community. Running a project is difficult enough, so you should avoid making unnecessary enemies.

> Make friends not war!

So, consult with the elders and leaders of the community. Seek their advice on how a group should be formed. They might not be too enthusiastic about doing anything! They might even have their own reasons for not wanting a group to be formed.

CALLING A COMMUNITY MEETING

The objective should be to try and persuade the community leaders to call a meeting so that everyone can have the opportunity to give their opinions and to decide on the next steps to be taken. If the leaders agree then let them call the meeting. If the leaders do not agree, ask their permission for those who have already shown an interest to arrange a meeting. If they do not agree with that request, then there is more than one problem! If this happens, those who want to proceed with a project must be completely honest with themselves when deciding what to do next. Is the original problem so important that it must be solved, even if it means upsetting some leaders of the community? The advice must be sought of members of the community who are respected and trusted. If all else fails, then the group must arrange a community meeting.

A community meeting should be held at the most convenient time and place. Avoid times when people have to work or be at another place, such as church, school or market. When deciding on the location, consideration should be given to how many people are likely to attend. If the meeting is to be held in the evening, light will be required. If the location is a school or church, permission will have to be obtained for its use.

> **Advertise:**
> **do not assume that everyone will know about the meeting**

This will be the first meeting of the group, so it is important to get as many people as possible to attend. The most effective way of advertising the meeting is by talking to people. Notices can also be put up around the community, and announcements made at church meetings and schools. People must be informed:

- Why the meeting is being held. Explain what the problem to be solved is. Show the people that they are also affected and that it would be to their advantage to attend. Make them feel that it is essential that they should attend.
- The day, time and place of the meeting.

To achieve an orderly meeting, someone who has the respect of those attending should be invited to act as the chairperson for the meeting.

All activities must have an objective. The objective of the meeting is to get all interested community members to join together to solve the problem. There is always the risk when people come together for the first time that they will try and solve 'all the world's problems at one time'. Do not be too ambitious at the first meeting. Before the meeting starts, everyone should know the objective of the meeting.

> **The reason for calling the first meeting**
> **is to form a group to solve the problem**

If a group is formed, the first step will have successfully been taken to solving the group's problem. Before the meeting closes, agreement should also be reached on the next step to be taken. Decide on the time, place and agenda (see page 27) for the next meeting.

> **Plan for your second meeting
> before the end of the first meeting**

Formation of a group

Now that members of the community have agreed to form a group, it must be organized to achieve the group's objectives. Most groups elect a committee to manage their affairs.

Is a committee necessary? What other ways are there?

One person can be appointed to run things. He or she can take all the decisions and do all the work. There are very few who have the skills, talents and energy to successfully achieve this.

Or, decisions can be taken and actions performed collectively by all members of the group. This is a practical solution for small groups. However, for larger groups this becomes more difficult to achieve. Also if the group has to deal with other organizations, they might require the group to identify spokespersons or contact persons.

In most cases, a group works more efficiently when it has a committee to manage and protect its interests. Members of the committee must always remember that they are there to:

- Carry out the wishes of the group.
- Work to achieve the objectives of the group.
- Consult and keep the group informed.
- Protect the interests of the group.
- Act in accordance with the group's constitution (see page 30).

When members elect the group committee, they should ignore whether a candidate is a friend, brother, sister, wife, cousin or any other relationship. The important thing is to be sure that candidates are capable of performing the duties of committee and executive members.

The group will need to appoint someone to run the elections, a Returning Officer. He or she should not be a candidate nor be seen to favour any one candidate over another. Your group will also have to decide whether the elections will be by secret ballot or show of hands. If you decide on a secret ballot, you will have to make arrangements for ballot papers.

Duties of the executive and committee members

A committee is normally made up of executive members: chairperson, secretary, treasurer and perhaps an assistant-chairperson, -secretary, -treasurer and ordinary committee members. In general their duties are as described below.

CHAIRPERSON

The chairperson is normally regarded by the group members as being their leader. As such, he/she has two important tasks to perform:

- The chairperson must not only be, but also be seen to be, the representative of the group. Within the group, that person has to provide leadership. He or she must also have the skills to represent the group in discussions with other organizations.
- The chairperson presides over group meetings and is responsible for ensuring that they are conducted in an orderly and businesslike manner.

To accomplish these duties, the chairperson should have certain leadership qualities and skills. He/she should be someone who:

- Is respected by the group and the committee members.
- Likes and understands people.
- Can get people to work well together.
- Behaves reasonably and respectfully even when vexed!
- Knows his/her own strengths and weaknesses.
- Is well informed, knows what is happening not only in the group, but also in the community at large.
- Is good at solving problems and making decisions.
- Takes action when necessary.

When presiding over meetings, a chairperson should:

- Call the meeting to order on time.
- Know how to run and control a meeting.
- Not try to force his/her views on the committee.
- Ensure that the members stick to the point under discussion.
- Ensure that everyone has a say and not allow one person to do all the talking!
- Ensure that all the facts are known and understood before a decision is taken (summarize discussions).
- Ensure that, after a decision is taken, everyone understands what must be done, when it must be done by, and by whom.The chairperson should never forget that he or she is the representative of the group and has a duty towards the

group. The chairperson should never use the position to promote his or her self-interest.

> **The chairperson should lead, not dictate**

SECRETARY

The secretary is considered to be the executive member responsible for administration. This is achieved by:

- Keeping an accurate record (minutes) of all committee and group meetings, detailing:
  - Dates of all meetings and place held
  - Names of those attending
  - Main points of the discussion
  - Decisions taken
  - Actions required to be taken and by whom.
- Sending and receiving all correspondence. To avoid confusion one person should be authorized to enter into correspondence on behalf of the group.
- Keeping safe all correspondence and group documents.

> **Keep all information and records safe:**
> **one day they could be important**

- Ensuring that the group has all the required legal approvals, permits and other documentation.

Example

If the group owns vehicles they will have to be insured and licensed. The distribution and handling of some chemicals used in farming might require permits. An entertainment licence might be required before a group can hold a dance or fund-raising show. If the group owns buildings and equipment, they should be insured against damage or loss.

> **Ensure that all licences, permits and insurance**
> **policies are valid and up-to-date**

TREASURER

As the executive member entrusted with the supervision of the group's financial affairs, the treasurer should:

- Keep safe all cash (money) held in hand. This is the petty cash fund, used to make small purchases and payments. A record of all these transactions should be made in a book kept specially for that purpose.
- Administer (look after) the money paid into and taken out of the group's bank account(s).
- Keep the accounts, an accurate (correct) record of all money received and paid by the group.
- Keep all receipts, invoices and bills, together with all financial records. While the accounts provide a record of financial transactions, receipts must be obtained to provide proof.

> Remember – it's the group's money

COMMITTEE MEMBERS

Committee members have an important role to play. They should not consider that only executive members have an active part to play in the running of the group. They must be prepared to:

- Discuss their ideas and make suggestions.
- Help the executive members to perform their duties.
- Check that the executive members are doing their work.
- Take full part in the work of the committee.
- Ensure that the group operates according to its constitution.

If the committee members do not perform their duties the group will suffer.

> A group is as good as its committee

GROUP MEMBERS

Some members think that all they have to do is elect the committee, then they can do nothing. A group gets the committee it deserves! If the members show little interest in the activities of the group, they should not be too surprised if the committee ignores their wishes. Group members must be prepared to:

- Take an active part in group activities.
- Keep informed of what is happening.
- Attend and **take part** in meetings.

- Select committee members because they are capable of doing the work, and not just because they are relatives or friends.
- Check that the committee is doing its work.
- **Help** the committee to do its work.
- Make certain that the group operates in accordance with its constitution (see page 30).

> The group gets the committee it deserves

Group meetings

Groups in general hold three types of meetings:

- *General meetings* which all the members of the group can attend and at which all may speak. At these meetings the committee reports on the group's activities. Decisions are taken on general group policy. Every year, or at agreed intervals, elections are held to select executive and committee members.
- *Committee meetings* at which the elected members of the committee can attend and speak. At these meetings, decisions are taken on the actions to be taken to achieve the group's objectives.
- *Executive meetings* at which the elected executive members can attend and speak. These meetings are normally held more often than the other two types, and decisions are taken on the day-to-day operations of the group.

In addition to the three types of meetings listed above, the group could decide to hold other types of meetings:

- *Emergency General Meetings* can be called when the committee or a group of members considers that urgent consideration of a subject is required by all the members.
- *Sub-committees* can be formed of experts to consider and look after the interests of the group on specialist subjects such as finance, buildings, welfare. The sub-committees should give reports, make recommendations and be answerable to the main committee.

WHY HAVE GROUP AND COMMITTEE MEETINGS?

Meetings:

- Give everyone the chance to **discuss** and give their views and ideas.
- Allow people with experience and knowledge to give advice.

- Bring together people to **discuss** and **think** of answers in order to solve problems.
- Bring together people to **discuss** and come to decisions and make plans.
- Allow reviews to be made of what has happened and **decisions** about what should be done next.
- Allow the executive members to obtain the help of committee members.
- Allow committee members to check that the executive members are doing their work properly.
- Are a means of providing and sharing information.
- Allow members to check that the group is operating in accordance with its constitution.

A great deal can be achieved or a lot of time wasted at meetings, depending upon how well they are run.

All meetings require a **quorum**, that is, a minimum number of members who must be present before the decisions taken at the meeting can be regarded as valid.

All the members have the responsibility to make sure that meetings are successful. This can be done by:

- Turning up on time for the meeting. When people do not arrive on time and keep other members waiting they are stealing people's time!
- Maintain good order in the meeting and respect the authority of the chairperson.
- Listen to other people's views and opinions.
- Participate in the meeting.
- Taking decisions based on the facts presented, and not out of fear, malice or favouritism.

The chairperson has the added responsibility for managing the meeting, by ensuring that:

- All those who wish to speak are given the opportunity to do so.
- The members concentrate on the subject under consideration, and the discussion does not wander off into irrelevant areas.
- When the time comes to take a decision, all those present know and understand the facts to be considered in reaching agreement. If a vote is required, this is taken democratically.
- After a decision has been taken the result is understood by all members. If required, those responsible for undertaking actions are identified.

Members may be too shy to speak in public. Some will require encouragement and assistance to boost their confidence, while others will remain too nervous to participate. This is no reason to fail to obtain their views. Before the meeting, committee members should try to obtain their opinions and report the results at the meeting. Some members, while being too shy to talk at a large meeting, might be prepared to give their views in a small discussion group. If during a large meeting, it becomes apparent that members are not participating, it may be a good idea to break the meeting up into small discussion groups. After the discussion, one person from each of the small groups can report back to the meeting.

MEETING AGENDA

To assist in the smooth running of a meeting it is best, before the meeting starts, to make out a list of the topics to be discussed at the meeting. This list is called the agenda. It can be written by the chairperson together with the secretary, and agreed to by those attending.

For a committee meeting the agenda could include the following.

COMMITTEE MEETING AGENDA		
1.	Announcements	
2.	Agenda	
3.	Minutes of previous meeting	
4.	Correspondence	
5.	Reports:	
	a)	Chairperson
	b)	Secretary
	c)	Treasurer
	d)	Any other
6.	Matters Arising	
7.	Any Other Business	
8.	Next meeting	

Announcements

Should include apologies for absence. Members who know that they cannot attend a meeting should send a message to the meeting. In this way, the committee's time can be saved, rather than waiting in vain for someone to turn up.

Agenda

While this might be written by the secretary and chairperson, the committee members should have the opportunity either to make changes or to approve it.

Minutes of previous meeting

The secretary should keep a record of all meetings (see over). At a meeting a copy of the minutes of the previous meeting should be made available to the committee members or the secretary should read them out. If anything is incorrect it should be changed. However, if some members believe that an incorrect decision was taken, the record cannot be changed. The decision should be raised for further discussion under 'Matters arising'. When everyone agrees that the minutes are correct they should be approved, and signed by the chairperson and secretary.

Correspondence

The secretary should read out all letters received by the group and all replies sent.

Reports

A meeting should be used to keep everyone informed of the activities of the group. This can be done by reports of the important events that have occurred since the last meeting.

Matters arising

Enables the members of the committee to discuss items that have arisen either in the minutes of the previous meeting, correspondence or reports. Members should use this opportunity to find out what progress has been made on decisions taken at previous meetings. If members want to reconsider a decision taken at the last meeting, this is the time and place to do it.

Any other business

This gives the opportunity for a member to raise any other topic, not covered in the meeting.

Next meeting

It is particularly useful, before a meeting closes, to agree on the time, date and place the next meeting will be held.

MINUTES OF MEETINGS

To avoid confusion and arguments it is best if a written record is kept of a meeting. These are known as the minutes and are normally kept by the secretary. They should contain a brief but accurate account of the discussions and decisions taken. If possible the minutes should be typed and each member provided with a copy. If copies cannot be made, or the minutes cannot be typed, they should be recorded in a Minutes Book kept specially for that purpose. The minutes of a typical committee meeting could contain the information shown in the illustration.

Minutes Of The [*name of group*], held on [*date*] at [*place meeting was held*].

1. **Present Were:** [*Names of those attending*]

2. **Announcements:** [*Details of apologies for absence*]

3. **Agenda:** [*i.e. The agenda was read by the chairperson and agreed by the committee*]

4. **Minutes of previous meeting:** [*Give details if there were any corrections and whether they were approved*]

5. **Correspondence:** [*Give brief details of letters received and sent*]

6. **Reports:**
   a) **Chairperson.**
   b) **Secretaries.** [*Give brief details of the most important points reported*]
   c) **Treasurers.**
   d) **Other Reports.**

7. **Matters Arising:** [*Give brief report on the main points discussed, and* **actions** *to be taken and by* **who**]

8. **Any Other Business:** [*Give brief report and record what* **actions** *are to be taken and by* **who**]

9. **Next Meeting:** [*State time, date and place*]

Qualities of a good leader

When a person accepts a place on the executive or committee they are taking on the responsibility of looking after the interests of the members of the group. Their duties do not finish with attending meetings; they must also take on the responsibilities of leadership.

There is a difference between managing your own business, where you can order people what to do, and being a leader of a group. Becoming a leader is not easy; it does not just happen by itself. Like all things it must be worked at! A leader of a group must earn the respect and trust of the members and should be good at working with people.

When working **with** people:

- Be friendly.
- Be helpful.
- Be honest – not only with others, but also with **yourself**.
- Be fair.
- Make people feel important.
- Keep your word.
- Do things on time.
- Pay your debts.
- Know what you are doing.
- Do as well as you can.

When leading people:

- Make sure that they know what you expect of them.
- Get everyone to work as a team, supporting each other.
- Watch that things are being done as was agreed.
- Do not criticize, give advice on how to improve.
- To get people to work well together:
  - Give praise.
  - Listen and ask for their advice and suggestions.
  - Give responsibility.
  - Treat everyone as individuals.
  - Treat everyone fairly.

> **Do unto others as you wish others to do unto you**

Group constitution and Standing Orders

It is likely that very soon after a group is formed, the need will arise for the members to agree on rules to govern how the group should be organized. At first they may state the size of the committee and how it is elected. As the number of group activities increase, so will the need for more rules. Especially before the group starts handling money, the members will have to agree and record a set of rules, which are known as the group's constitution.

- Normally the first clause of the constitution is called the 'preamble' and is of the form:

  '*{Name of the group} hereafter referred to as the "Group" hereby adopts and sets forth this Constitution*'

The group constitution could contain the following:

1.	The name of the group and preamble.	
2.	The objectives of the group.	*What are the general and specific objectives of the group.*
3.	Group membership.	*Who can become a member, and will there be a membership fee.*
4.	Management of the group.	*Size of the committee. Executive members and their duties. How is the committee elected and for how long do the members serve.*
5.	Operation of the group.	*Rules governing the day to day operation of the group. Stating how standing orders are approved. The rules for the management of group employees.*
6.	Meetings.	*The holding of committee, executive and general meetings. The calling of emergency general meetings. Quorum of meetings (how many members must be present before a meeting can be held).*
7.	Finance.	*The administration of the group's bank account. Who can sign cheques. Can the groups money be used to give private loans.*
8.	Constitution.	*The procedures for changing and adding to the constitution.*

- The second clause should define both the general and specific objectives of the group.
- Every constitution should have a clause defining the procedures that must be followed when approving amendments to it.

The objectives of the Group are:

  i)   To provide a safe and economic boat transport service for the community.

  ii) To use any profits made, to provide loans to the members of the Group.

The constitution is an important document. It states clearly who can become a member of the group, and also how the group is managed. It is the protection the members have to prevent any small sub-group from taking over the group and its *assets*. As such the constitution itself must be protected from those who might want to take over the group. One way of doing this is by stating that the constitution cannot be amended unless the proposed amendment is approved by a majority of *all* the members of the group.

The constitution sets out the fundamental principles governing the operation of the group. As such, these 'golden rules' should only be changed when absolutely necessary. There are other rules that the group might require as guidelines for members to conduct the day-to-day operations of the group. These rules, known as the Standing Orders, can be changed to suit circumstances.

Example

If the group owns equipment which it hires out to members (e.g. a chainsaw, sewing machine, boat), Standing Orders could be used to state the hire charge, the maximum time it can be hired by a member, who is responsible for maintaining it, and so on.

Business letter writing

Probably the first way the group will make contact with other organizations will be by sending a business letter. It is important that it gives a good impression. Before starting to write a letter:

- Think out your reasons for sending the letter and what you hope to achieve by it.
- Make a list of what you want to say.

When writing the letter:

- State the objectives clearly.
- Avoid using big or 'fancy' words. Be as straight forward as you can.
- Write neatly. If possible, type the letter.
- Keep a copy of all letters sent.

The layout of a business letter is as shown in the illustration and as described overleaf.

```
                                    Fumisua Development
                                    Group,
                                    c/o R. S. Small,
                                    FUMISUA,
       IICA,                        Region 11.
       PO Box 10 - 1089,
       GEORGETOWN.                  15th, July 1999

       Dear Sir

              REQUEST FOR TRAINING PROGRAMME
```

- Write the group's address in the top right hand corner.
- Just below, on the left hand side of the page, write the name and address of the person you are writing to. If you are writing to a company or organization use the company's name.
- On the right hand side of the page write the date.
- On the left hand side, below the address of the receiver, write the salutation (the greeting).

There are rules for the use of salutations for business letters.

- If you **know** the person you are writing to, start the letter with:
    Dear *Mr {Name of person}*,
    or
    Dear *Miss {Name of person}*,
    or
    Dear *Mrs {Name of person}*,
    or
    Dear *Ms {Name of person}* – if you are not sure about the marital status of a woman.
- If you **do not** know the person you are writing to, start the letter with:
    Dear Sir,
    or
    Dear Madam,

Just below the salutation, in the centre of the page, write the title of the letter. This should be a very short sentence describing the main reason for writing, for example, 'Application for loan', 'Request for the use of the school to hold a meeting', etc.
   The first paragraph of the letter should state the reason for the letter:

Example

I write to you on behalf of the Fumisua Development Group. We are seeking assistance to run training programmes in project and small business management.

The next paragraph(s) should give additional information:

Example

Our group was formed last year and has 200 members. To date we have successfully completed the following projects . . . etc.

The last paragraph should clearly state how you wish the receiver to respond to the letter:

Example

In order to discuss our request, we would appreciate it if you could grant representatives of the group an appointment with you at your earliest convenience. Please notify us about the details of the appointment in good time so that we can make all necessary arrangements.

As with the salutation, there are rules governing the closing courtesy used in a business letter. The closing courtesy should be written on the left hand side just below the last paragraph.

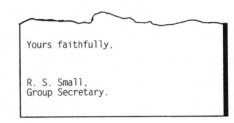

```
Yours faithfully,


R. S. Small,
Group Secretary.
```

- If you **know** the person you are writing to, close the letter with:

    Yours **sincerely**

- If you **do not** know the person you are writing to, close the letter with:

    Yours **faithfully**

Sign the letter below the closing courtesy. Often it is difficult to read a person's signature, so to assist the reader, print below the signature your name and title, i.e. Group Secretary, Chairperson, etc.

> Keep a copy of **all** letters sent.

Questions and exercises

These questions and exercises have been designed to assist participants to organize themselves into a group.

You are advised to read the beginning of this chapter before attempting the following exercises and questions.

THE FIRST STEP

Question: What is the problem the group wants to solve?

Question: How many residents of the community are affected?

Question: Are some residents affected more than others?

Exercise: *Make a list of all the people who will be interested in joining together to solve the problem.*

Question: Who should you discuss the problem with first?

Question: Who are the elders and leaders of the community?

Question: How can you get their assistance?

Question: Who are the people you respect who can give advice on how to organize a group?

Seek supporters

CALLING A COMMUNITY MEETING

Question: What is the best day to hold a community meeting?

Question: What is the best time to hold a community meeting?

Question: Where is the best place to hold the meeting?

Question: Who is responsible for the proposed meeting place?

Question: Will permission be required to use it?

Question: What is the best way of informing all the community about the meeting?

Encourage people to attend the meeting

Exercise:	*Design a poster to advertise the meeting. What details will have to be included?*
Question:	Who is the best person to act as the chairperson for the meeting?
Question:	Does he or she have the respect of the people who are likely to attend the meeting?
Question:	Who should ask that person to act as the chairperson?
Question:	What do you hope to achieve by holding a meeting?
Question:	Should there be an agenda for the meeting?
Question:	What are the objectives of the meeting?
Exercise:	*List the order in which items should be discussed at the meeting.*
Question:	What is the best time and place for the next meeting?

> **The first objective is to form a group**

FORMATION OF A GROUP

Question:	Does the group require a committee?
Question:	How do you decide what is the correct number of members for a committee?
Question:	How many members should the committee have?
Question:	Should there be an executive committee?
Question:	How many members should it have?
Question:	What will be their duties?
Question:	How should the committee be elected: at a group meeting or a specially arranged election?
Question:	How are the committee members to be elected: by secret ballot or by show of hands?
Question:	Who is going to run the elections, take the nominations and count the votes etc?

DUTIES OF THE EXECUTIVE AND COMMITTEE MEMBERS

Exercise: *Make a list of the most important qualities fo a chairperson. Place them in order of importance.*

Exercise: *Make a list of individuals who would be a good chairperson.*

> ## The chairperson must be trustworthy

Exercise: *Write, in the order of importance, the most important qualities of a secretary.*

Exercise: *Make a list of the individuals who would make a good secretary.*

Question: What are the most important qualities of a treasurer?

Exercise: *Write a list of the individuals who would make a good treasurer.*

Exercise: *Write a list, in the order of importance, of the most important qualities members of the committee will require.*

Exercise: *Make a list of the people who would make good committee members.*

> ## The group is only as good as its members

GROUP MEETINGS

Why have group and committee meetings?

Question: What are the three most important reasons for having meetings?

Exercise: *You are the chairperson of a meeting. One person or a small group of persons is doing all the talking and trying to force their views onto the group. The other members present are not taking part. What can you do to encourage the other members to give their views?*

Question: When people are too nervous to speak in a big group, would it be a good idea to split the meeting up into small discussion groups?

Question: How can the meeting know what took place in each small group?

Question: What other ways can be used to get people to take part in a meeting?

Question: What are the three most important qualities of a good chair-person of a meeting?

Question: Why have sub-committees?

Question: Would it be useful for your group to have sub-committees?

Question: Can only committee members be members of a sub-committee or can other people with special skills and experience be invited to join?

Meeting agenda and minutes

Exercise: *Write out an agenda for a general meeting of a group.*

Question: At general meetings, should executive members be required to give a report on their activities?

Exercise: *At a committee meeting the secretary reads out the minutes of the last meeting. His record is wrong and he has failed to record a number of important decisions taken. Should the minutes be corrected? How can this be done?*

Exercise: *At a meeting the secretary reads out the minutes of the last meeting. One of the members, who was not present at the meeting, disagrees with one of the decisions that had been taken. Some of the other members agree with her and she tries to get the minutes changed. If the majority of the committee agree, should the minutes be changed?*

Question: Is it correct that minutes should always be an accurate record of a meeting? And should they be corrected if they are wrong?

Question: Is it correct to say that minutes should not be changed to give a false report of what happened at a meeting?

Question: If someone disagrees with the decision taken at the previous meeting, can the subject be discussed again under 'Matters arising' and a new vote taken?

Question: What is the minimum number of members required to request the calling of an emergency general meeting?

Question: Is it essential that all the members of the group be notified when an emergency general meeting is called?

Question: How long will it take to inform all the members of the group of the time and place where an emergency general meeting will be held?

Question: Should there be a clause in the group's constitution to state the minimum number of members required to call an emergency general meeting, and the minimum notice given before it is held?

> Emergency meetings should not be called irresponsibly

Question: What does the word 'quorum' mean?

Question: Should there be a minimum number of members present before a committee meeting or general meeting can be held?

Question: What should be the minimum number of committee members present before a committee meeting can be held, a quarter, one-third, a half or two-thirds of the committee?

Question: What should the quorum be for a general meeting, more or less than a quarter of the total number of members?

QUALITIES OF A GOOD LEADER

Exercise: List five main differences between the qualities required by a business manager and those of a group leader.

Question: Will someone who is a successful business man/woman always be a good leader of a group?

Question: Why is it important to 'be honest with yourself'?

Exercise: Think of all the bosses you have had, and leaders you have known. Make a list of all their good and bad qualities.

Question: What are the five most important qualities of a good leader?

Question: What qualities do bad leaders have?

Exercise: You are a leader of a group. You ask one of the members to do a simple job. When you check on the work you find that he has done it all wrong! What should you do?

(a) Give him a telling off and tell him that he must go back and do the work again.

(b) Correct the work yourself or get someone else to do it and make a note never to ask him to do any work again!

(c) Talk nicely to him and point out that he did not do a very

38

good job. Then explain to him how you want the job done, and that you are giving him another chance to do it.

(d) Ask yourself whether, when you gave him the instructions, you explained clearly what was required, and checked that he had understood them. If you are in the wrong, go and apologize to him for not giving him the correct instructions.

(e) Ask yourself, if you had done something wrong, how you would want a good leader to treat you?

Question: What can you do to make people feel important?

GROUP CONSTITUTION AND STANDING ORDERS

Question: What is the main difference between the purpose of a group's constitution and its Standing Orders?

Exercise: *Which of the following topics should be included in the group's constitution and which in the Standing Orders?*

(a) Rules governing the number of members on the committee and how long they should hold office.

(b) Who can become a member of the group.

(c) The amount of the group's membership fee.

(d) How often group general meetings should be held.

(e) How often the executive should meet.

(f) That the group's funds, above a certain limit, should be held in the group's bank account.

(g) The names of the persons who will administer the bank account.

(h) Rules controlling the use of the group's equipment.

Question: Why should the constitution only be changed infrequently?

Question: Should the committee be able to change the constitution, or should it only be done by a vote of the members of the group?

Question: If the constitution can only be changed by a vote taken at a general meeting of the group, can it be done by a simple majority or should it require a higher number of votes? Should two-thirds or three-quarters of the members present vote for the change?

> Protect the constitution

BUSINESS LETTER WRITING

Question: What is the postal address of the group?

Question: Who should write and sign group letters, the chairperson, the secretary or either person?

Question: If you know the person you are writing to, do you start the letter, Dear Sir or Dear {Name of the person you are writing to}?

Question: What closing courtesy should be used when writing to someone you **do not** know?

Question: Why should you print your name and title under your signature?

Exercise: *Write a letter to the headteacher asking permission to use the school to hold a general meeting of the group, next Friday at 6.00 p.m.*

A letter presents an image of the group

CHAPTER 3

Solution identification and planning

The problem has been identified and a group of people have organized themselves to do something about it. Now how can the group proceed to solve the problem?

> ### Seek advice and assistance

A lot of time and effort can be saved by a group if they seek help and advice from people who have skills and experience in solving problems. These can be people in the community who have previously managed community development projects or outside organizations who run training programmes.

Training

The group can organize training workshops to strengthen their management and organizing skills. These can be run using trainers from within the community or from external organizations. Whoever is used, a commitment will be required, certainly by the group committee and interested group members, to attend the training sessions. If people are expected to give up their time, then the training provided must be relevant.

> ### What is taught is what is required
> ### and what is required is what is taught

It is important before any training starts that the group discuss and examine their training needs with the trainers, and together design the content of the training programme to meet the immediate needs of the group. It is likely that those attending the workshops are adults who have not attended school for some years and have many responsibilities. They will not be eager to sit in a classroom for long periods. Training sessions should therefore not be too long. Also, not too many sessions should be held each week. There is no need to have all the training at one time. The sessions can be organized to take place at appropriate times throughout the period of the project.

> Training must be relevant
> and what is learnt put
> immediately into practice

> Now that a group has been formed,
> repeat the analysis of the problem –
> all the group members must agree
> on the problem they are going to solve

Setting objectives

Remember, the group was organized with the objective of solving a problem. Many projects fail because inappropriate solutions are applied to problems. This happens when the answer is identified before the question!

Example

An aid agency decided to provide a village with a water system. They installed a pump driven by a petrol engine, to pump water from the river up to two large plastic tanks installed on a wooden tower, built in the middle of the village. The women and children no longer had to walk down to the river to fetch their water, but would go daily to the tower to fill their buckets. For the first few months things went well. Then the supply of petrol provided by the aid agency finished. The Village Council decided that in future, to enable them to buy petrol, they would make a small charge for each bucket of water. While some women decided that they could pay, most of the women went back to getting their water from the river. Because so few people were using the pumped water the charge had to be increased. There were a lot of complaints and grumbling. Soon the dry season started. Since the village was only a short distance from the mouth of the river, salt water would flow up from the sea to the village. So the pumps could not be used. At the end of the dry season the two tanks were removed from the tower and placed next to the school where they were used to store the rain water falling off the roof. The pump was never used again!

A villager calculated that for the money the aid agency had spent on the pump, pipes and building the tower, they could have provided each house in the village with its own storage tank!

In the above example, the aid agency had their answer first. They did not ask the question whether the villagers could afford to run and maintain the pump, or even whether the river was a reliable source of clean fresh water.

Do not fall into the same trap of choosing an answer before you fully understand the question.

> The success of the project will depend upon
> selecting the right solution:
> do not be too hasty in choosing an answer

Objectives analysis

In Chapter 1, methods were described of how to identify a problem. Once this has been done an objective can be set.

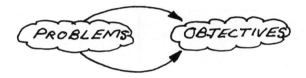

During objectives analysis the problems are converted into objectives towards which activities can be directed. It also includes examining the objectives to see if they are practical and achievable.

The analysis is performed in five steps:

- All the negative problems are restated as positive objectives.
- The objectives are then examined to ensure that they are both desirable, realistic and achievable in an acceptable time frame.
- The objectives that do not meet the conditions mentioned above are modified, while those that are undesirable or cannot be achieved are dropped.
- Any new objectives identified during the analysis are added.
- The overall relationships and interactions between the problems and objectives are examined to ensure that they are true, make sense and cover all likely possibilities.

If a defined problem cannot be easily converted into a positive, objective statement, it may indicate that the problem has not been clearly identified, and the problem requires further examination.

Let us apply this procedure to the example given in Chapter 1.

Example

For some years the mains water supply pipeline has been out of service. Households have had to rely on storing rain water. It is now the dry season. Last week the last of the water was used from the storage tank.

The 'problem tree' derived was:

GARDEN PLANTS DYING.	***** *This effect was identified during the preparation of the problem tree.*

NO WATER TO WASH	NO WATER FOR BATHING AND WASHING CLOTHES	NO WATER TO WATER GARDEN.

NO WATER SUPPLY FOR THE HOUSE. (CORE PROBLEM).

MAINS WATER SUPPLY IS OUT OF ORDER.	WATER STORAGE TANK IS EMPTY.	CREEK WATER IS SALTY.

MAINS WATER SUPPLY PIPELINE BROKEN FOR 10 YEARS!	DURING THE DRY SEASON SEA WATER FLOWS UP THE CREEK

NO RAIN FOR 3 MONTHS	STORAGE TANK TOO SMALL!

Converting the problems into objectives, the 'objectives tree' would be:

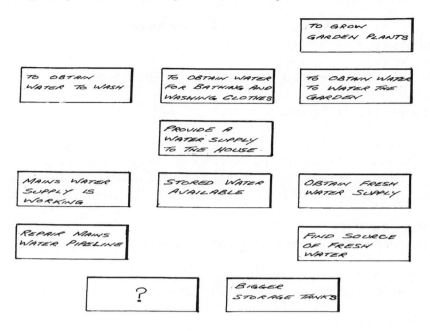

If the problem analysis chart method is used, the result is:

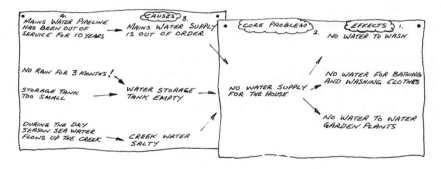

With a resulting objective analysis chart:

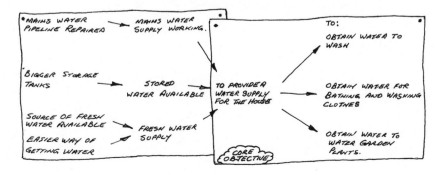

Notice that the 'core problem' has been converted from:

'No water supply for the house'

to the 'core objective':

'To provide a water supply for the house'.

Objective statements always start with the word '**to**'.

In the above example, what are the problems that have to be solved? One problem certainly is that during the dry season, the creek that supplies the village with water turns salty. There might also be a further problem: during the dry season, the women and children have to walk too far to collect water from another source.

So the first problem *is:*
   The lack of fresh water during the dry season.

The first objective *is:*
   To provide fresh water during the dry season.

The second problem *is:*
   The women and children have to walk too far to fetch water.

The second objective *is:*
   To provide an easier way of getting water.

The second objective could have been identified as: *To provide a source of water supply closer to the village.* However, stating the objective in this way is indicating an answer, by suggesting that some source other than the creek should be used. We will see later how this narrows down the number of solutions to the problem.

> Avoid looking for solutions
> when identifying objectives

Identifying solutions

Before starting to look for solutions, list all the problems and objectives. Also agree upon their order of importance.

Once the objectives have been agreed on, a start can be made to identify all possible practical solutions. It is important when identifying a solution not to choose your 'favourite' solution too quickly, but to keep an open mind. One method of doing this is called 'brain storming' which is done as follows.

- The group committee, and other members who can assist, hold a meeting.
- A time limit is set, say 15 minutes, for each person working on their own to write down, for each objective, all the solutions they can think of. People should be as imaginative as possible. It does not matter how crazy or impossible the solution might seem, it should be written down. (If people cannot write, get them to make simple drawings.)
- Then, using a blackboard and chalk or a flip chart and felt marker, list all the solutions identified. At this stage people should try to avoid discussing or passing comments on the solutions.
- After seeing what solutions other people have thought of, each person again working on his or her own, tries to think of more solutions. After the set time is up, these new solutions are added to the list.
- Work through the list and decide which of the solutions are possible and which are impossible. Again try to avoid choosing the solution too quickly.

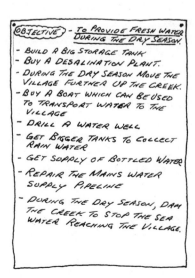

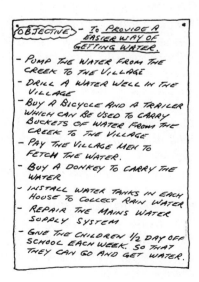

The result of a brain storming session for this example could be:

For objective 1   To provide fresh water during the dry season.

and objective 2   To provide an easier way of getting water.

Of course, more solutions can be identified than the few listed in the examples shown.

At this stage the group should consider something that was ignored by the aid agency in the example at the beginning of this chapter:

SUSTAINABILITY – that is, the ability of the project to continue to provide a solution to the problem for as long as is required.

It will be seen in Chapter 5 that sustainability is a critical factor considered by funding agencies when deciding whether to make a loan or give a grant to a group to fund a project. Attention must not only be given to the implementation, but also to the long-term running and maintenance of the project. It was seen in the example that one of the reasons the project failed was that the villagers could not afford to buy fuel for the engine. They also did not have the necessary mechanical skills to maintain it.

The next stage in selecting the solution is to consider the sustainability of the solutions identified. Even at this stage, try not to make a final selection of a solution. Keep open as many options as possible.

The result of examining some of the options for the above example is:

- *Build a big storage tank to store the fresh creek water.*
  - *The tank will have to be large enough to store water for all the village for the whole period of the dry season.*
  - *Once installed it will have low running and maintenance costs.*
  - *Where should it be built – close to the creek or in the village?*

- *Drill a new water well in the village.*
  - *The cost of drilling a well could be very high.*
  - *How deep will it have to be?*
  - *Will it require a motor-driven pump, or could a hand-operated pump work?*
  - *The well could be drilled right in the middle of the village.*

- *Buy a donkey to carry the water.*
  - *Someone will have to be paid to look after it.*
  - *When not carrying water, it could be used to transport other things for the village. Hire charges could be obtained.*
  - *A new donkey would have to be bought when it dies.*

- *Repair the mains water supply pipeline.*
  - *The Water Authority will have to repair and restore their water well, water treatment plant and pumps.*
  - *This will be a very large and expensive project, which the government will have to manage.*
  - *The system will have high running and maintenance costs.*

It can be seen from the above four options that when a solution is examined for sustainability, the results can be positive or negative, or you are left with more questions to answer! By this stage a solution can be classed as:

- **Practical, and it will solve the problem.**
- **Might be practical and it might solve the problem.**
- **Clearly will *not* solve the problem, and can be ignored.**

The solutions in the first two classes can be further examined by asking the following questions:

- **Will it (the solution) work?**
  It's all right having a good idea, but in practice will it work?
- **Will the members of the group work it?**
  Many projects have failed, because for one reason or another the group members failed to support it.

There are examples where water wells have been drilled, and remain unused as the people prefer the taste of the river water.

Or where items of equipment have been purchased, but soon failed because no one was prepared to take the trouble to maintain and clean them. It was always the case of 'Why should I do it? Let someone else do it'.

- **Is the solution worth doing?**
  The solution could cause bigger problems than the problem it was initially meant to solve.

To help villagers improve their standard of living, an overseas church group provided a tractor so that the villagers could increase the production from their farms. There were four churches in the village. The tractor was given for the use of the members of one of the churches. The result was jealousy and quarrelling, in what had previously been a peaceful village.

> Examine project proposals
> to ensure that the project
> does not cause bigger problems
> than the problem it was trying to solve

- **Can the solution be seen to make things better, or start to make things better?**
  It does not matter how good the solution is, it will only work if the people help to make it work. People will only take the trouble to do this if they can see that they will benefit.

> People will not help to make the project succeed
> unless they can see that it is relevant to them

By this stage all the options should have been thoroughly examined and the list narrowed down to one or two solutions.

Identifying project actions

Solutions can be regarded as the outline. The details have to be added. These are the actions.

One of the solution options for the above example was:
'Build a big storage tank to store the fresh creek water'.
The list of actions to achieve this could include:
- *Decide where the tank should be built – by the creek or in the village.*
- *Decide on the size of the tank.*
- *Decide what materials should be used to build the tank.*
- *Decide on the method of filling the tank.*
- *Obtain the land to build the tank on.*
- *Design the tank and filling system.*
- *Buy the materials.*
- *Build the foundations for the tank.*
- *Build the tank.*
- *Construct the filling system.*
- *Test the tank and filling system.*

When considering the task, the above is just a part of the list of the actions that would have to be taken.

Project planning

When planning a project, a similar action list has to be made for all options still being considered.

PLANNING is thinking out and then working out in detail what has to be done and how it has to be done.

When planning, ask:

- **What has to be done?**
- **How is it to be done?**
- **What is needed?**
- **Who will do it?**
- **When is it to be done?**
- **How long will it take?**

> The project plan is not only used at the planning stage:
> it is the route map used throughout the project
> as a guide and a check that project activities
> are proceeding as required

A good planner can identify the likely problems that could occur during the project and plan to prevent them happening.

Planning is matching together activities, time and resources.

When preparing a project plan, examine each activity and ask:

- **What has to be done first?**
- **What activities can be done at the same time?**
- **What will be done next?**

The stages to be followed in preparing a project plan:

- **Make a list of all activities.**
- **Place them in the order that they should occur.**
- **Estimate how long each activity should take.**
- **Decide whether more than one activity can be undertaken at the same time.**

For example, for the building of a big storage tank to store fresh creek water, the following project activities would be necessary. The estimated number of days needed for each activity is given in brackets.

1 Conduct a survey to determine how many people will use the tank, how

51

much water they require and where they would prefer the tank to be built (15)

2 Look for suitable plot of land (5)
3 Purchase land (100)
4 Design tank (20)
5 Make list of materials required (2)
6 Make list of methods that can be used to fill tank (1)
7 Examine each method to see if it is sustainable (5)
8 Consult with group members, and make choice of method (5)
9 Design system for filling the tank (10)
10 Make list of materials required to build filling system (2)
11 Purchase materials (25)
12 Ask for cost estimates for building the tank and filling system (20)
13 Examine cost estimates, and choose contractor (5)
14 Give contract for building the tank and filling system (3)
15 Build tank and filling system (30)
16 Test tank and filling system (10)

The total number of days estimated is 258. But some of the activities can be done at the same time, for example, activity 4 – Design tank (20), and activity 6 – Make list of methods that can be used to fill tank (1).

Some activities cannot start until other activities have finished: for example, activity 4 – Design tank (20) must finish before a start can be made on activity 5 – Make list of materials required (2).

It is easier to place activities in order and decide what can or cannot be done at the same time if a 'bar chart' is used to give a visual representation of the project plan.

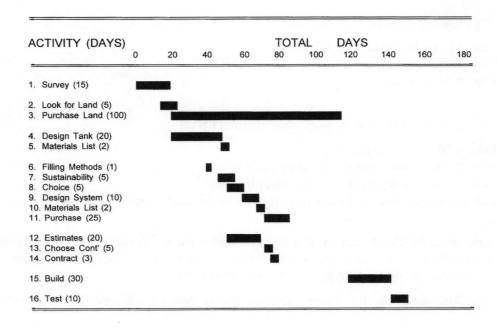

52

It can be seen from the bar chart that a number of activities can be performed at the same time. All the design, purchasing of materials and the employment of a contractor can be completed by day 88. The project is delayed by the time it takes to purchase the land, which has to be completed before the building work can start. The whole project is completed in 160 days.

Projects are easier to plan and manage if they are organized into smaller 'part' projects. In the above example, the part projects could be:

- *The survey.*
- *Selecting and purchasing the land.*
- *Designing the tank and compiling the list of materials.*
- *Designing the filling system and purchasing the materials.*
- *Selecting and employing the contractor.*
- *Building and testing the system.*

Planning for change

Things are always changing

Do not just leave things to happen. Plan and manage change. The group is undertaking the project to solve a problem; they are working to change things. The group members hope that as a result of the project things will be better. But this might not be so for all the community members; some will remain unaffected while others might be disadvantaged! Projects can bring bad as well as good results to a community. Do not just wait for things to go wrong: work to prevent problems from occurring. This will require thought to be given to future events and results, and planning to make sure things do not go wrong.

When planning a project, consider:

- **What are going to be the effects of the project?**
- **How will things change?**
- **What is going to happen?**

A solution should not be chosen
if it has an overall bad effect on the community

Group commercial projects

The example given above is of a community project which could improve the quality of life of the residents. Other group projects could be undertaken to improve the members' money earning ability. This will require preparing a business plan for the proposed business.

> A **BUSINESS PLAN** is an estimate of the future sales, costs and profit which can be achieved. It consists of a **SALES PLAN** and an **EXPENDITURE PLAN**.

> The objective of a business is to make a profit

A business must be run so that it is sustainable. It must make a profit in order not only to pay the running costs but also to provide money which can be used to help the business to grow.

> The business plan is used
> not only at the initial planning stage,
> to determine if the business is going to make a profit,
> but at each stage of the project to monitor
> whether the business is achieving the required results

In preparing a business plan you must decide:

- **How much do you want to sell ?**
- **How will you do it ?**
- **How long will it take ?**

In estimating the **sales** you must decide how many products you will want to sell:

- For a farm project this will require you to decide what crops will be grown and how much.
- For a craft or manufacturing project, what will be made and how many.

Estimate for every month:

- How many products you will sell.
- The price you will sell them for.
- Multiply the number sold by the price, this gives the **sales**.

The estimates for every month will give the SALES PLAN for the business. Adding up the sales for every month will give the TOTAL SALES for the period. (In the case of a farm project, there might not be sales every month but only at harvest time.)

To estimate the **costs** of running the business, make out a list, for every month, of the expected costs for running the business. Items that could be included are:

- Cost of purchasing materials.
- Labour costs (hired, self and family).
- Rental charges.
- Electricity and other fuel costs.
- Interest paid on loans.
- Transportation costs.
- Taxes.
- Repairs and replacement of equipment.
- Miscellaneous.

The estimates for every month will give the EXPENDITURE PLAN for the business.

Adding up all the expenses for each month will give the TOTAL EXPENDITURE for the period (one year or, in the case of a farm project, perhaps longer, depending on the crops cultivated).

> Profit = Sales − Expenditure

Taking away the **total expenditure** from the **total sales** gives the **total profit** for the period. As well as calculating the total profit for the period, the monthly estimates should be used to determine the 'cash flow' of the business. If, for a month, the sales are larger than the costs, money will be flowing into the business: '**positive cash flow**'. However if the costs are greater than the sales, money will be flowing out of the business, '**negative cash flow**', and for that month funds will have to be found to keep the business running.

> Before starting a commercial project,
> the group should seek specialist advice
> and training in small business management

Questions and exercises

These questions and exercises have been formulated in order to assist participants to set project objectives, identify solutions and then plan project activities. It is suggested that you read Chapters 1 and 3 before attempting them.

TRAINING

Question: What skills will the group require to plan and manage a project?

Question: Do the group members have those skills?

Question: Are there members in the community with those skills, who can train the group members?

Exercise: *Make a list of all the people who will be prepared to help train the group members, and the subjects they can provide training in.*

NAME	SUBJECTS
- ANN SMITH	- BOOK-KEEPING & ACCOUNTANCY.
- EDWARD CHARLES	- TRACTOR DRIVER & POWER SAW OPERATOR
- JOHN GIBBONS	- WAS CHAIRMAN OF SCHOOL BUILDING PROJECT GROUP.

Question: Will the group require the assistance of outside organizations to help run training programmes?

Exercise: *Make a list of all the subjects in which the group will require training.*

Question: How many of the committee and group members would be prepared to attend training workshops?

Question: What is the best day in the week to hold workshops?

Question: What is the best time during the day to hold workshops?

Question: Where can the workshops be held?

Question: Will the meeting place be available at the required time?

Question: Whose permission will be required to use the meeting place for the workshop?

> **Encourage members to participate**

SETTING OBJECTIVES

Question: Why is it important that all the group members are given the opportunity to review, and then agree on, the problem they are going to solve?

Question: How can the group reach agreement on the problem to be solved?

Question: What is the problem the group wants to solve?

Exercise: *Make a list of all the problems. Place them in order of importance.*

Question: What should come first, looking for the answer (solution) for each problem or deciding what the objectives are for each problem?

Question: What are the disadvantages of trying to identify the solution to the problem too quickly?

Question: What is the advantage of identifying the objectives before rushing to select a solution?

Exercise: *Examine the group's list of problems, and for each problem decide upon an objective.*

Question: What is the project's 'core objective'?

> Be sure that the correct objectives have been identified

IDENTIFYING SOLUTIONS

Question: What is meant by 'brain storming'?

Question: When first writing out the list of solutions, why should the participants try to avoid discussing or passing comments?

Question: How can members be encouraged to be as imaginative as possible when thinking up solutions?

Question: Are there some other methods the group can use to think of solutions?

Exercise: *Examine the list of objectives, and for each one make out a list of **all** the solutions the group can think of.*

'Let's give a prize to the person who thinks of the best solution'

Question: What is meant by 'sustainability'?

Exercise: *Make a list of all the factors that should be considered when examining whether the group's project solutions are sustainable.*

Exercise: *Examine the list of all the solutions and decide which would give a sustainable solution to the problem.*

Exercise: *Examine the list of sustainable solutions, and decide which are 'practical' solutions.*

Exercise: *Examine the list of practical solutions and decide whether the group members would support and actually use the solution.*

Exercise: *Examine the list and decide, for each solution, whether it could cause bigger problems in the community than the initial problem it is meant to solve.*

Exercise: *Finally, decide which solutions will really make things better.*

IDENTIFYING PROJECT ACTIONS

Question: After examining all the solutions, how many suitable solutions remain on your list?

Exercise: *For each of the remaining solutions make out a list of all the activities that must be undertaken in order to put the solution in place.*

PROJECT PLANNING

Question: Why prepare a project plan?

Question: Is a project plan used only during the planning stage of a project?

Exercise: *Examine the list of activities for the remaining solutions and put them into the order they should occur.*
Estimate how long each activity should take. Can some activities take place at the same time?

Question: What is a 'bar chart' and how can it be used to help to plan a project?

Exercise: *Prepare a bar chart for each of the remaining solutions.*

Hint Write the list of activities down the left hand side of the page.

Choose the scale to be used to represent the time for each activity; that is, the length of each bar on the bar chart. For example, if the scale of 1 inch (or, say, 2 cm) represents a month of activity, then an activity lasting two months would be represented by a bar 2 inches (4 cm) long. An activity which would last one week would be represented by a bar a quarter of an inch (5mm) long.

Decide which activities can be performed at the same time and which ones have to wait for another activity to be completed before they can start.

Exercise: *Examine the bar chart and decide which are the key activities that will determine how long the project will take.*

PLANNING FOR CHANGE

Question: Why is it important to plan for change?

Question: Are projects bound to give good results?

Question: If the majority of the community will benefit and only a small minority will suffer as a result of a project, should the well-being of the minority be ignored for the sake of the majority?

Question: Will the solution the group has chosen result in disruption in the community?

Question: What can be done to prevent a project having a bad effect on the community?

GROUP COMMERCIAL PROJECTS

Question: What should be achieved by a commercial project?

Question: Should a commercial project always make a profit?

Question: Does the group propose to manage a commercial project?

Question: What skills will a group require to plan and manage a commercial project?

Question: Do the group members have those skills?

Question: Are there members in the community with those skills, who can train the group members?

Exercise: *Make a list of all the people who will be prepared to help train the group members, and the subjects they can provide training in.*

Question: Will the group require the assistance of outside organizations to run training programmes?

Question: What is a business plan?

Question: How can a business plan be used when making decisions during the design of a project?

Question: Is a business plan used only during the design stage of a project?

Question: How can a business plan be used to see if a commercial project is meeting its objectives?

Question: What is a sales plan?

Question: What product(s) will the group be selling?

Question: How much of each product will be sold every month?

Question: What price will be charged for each product?

Question: What will be the total sales each month?

Question: What will be the total sales for the period?

Question: What is an expenditure plan?

Question: Will the project (business) be employing staff?

Question: What materials need to be purchased for the business each month?

Question: Will the business have to pay rent for the use of land or buildings?

Question: Will the group have to transport its products to market?

Exercise: *Make a list of the items of expenditure required for the running of the group's business project.*

Question: What will be the total cost of running the business every month?

Question: What period is covered by the plan – how many months?

Question: What is the total cost of running the business for the period?

Question: Will the business project make a profit for the period?

Question: What is 'positive cash flow'?

Question: What is 'negative cash flow'?

Question: During the period will there be any months with negative cash flow?

Question: What is the total amount of funds the business will require to pay running costs during the months with negative cash flow?

> **Seek training in business management**

CHAPTER 4

Resource identification and cost estimating

Resource identification

The use of project plans to identify the activities required to achieve project objectives is described in Chapter 3. To do what needs to be done, human, material and equipment resources will be required. Information can be obtained from the project plan to assist in preparing a list of those resources.

As an aid in identifying the resources you will need, a project resources form can be drawn up. Examples of all the appropriate forms appear at the end of this chapter.

ACTIVITIES	RESOURCES					
	Qty	HUMAN	Qty	EQUIPMENT	Qty	MATERIALS
(1)		(2)		(3)		(4)

Step 1

Using the project plan to identify all the project activities, list these in column 1 of the project resources form.

Step 2

Examine each of the activities in turn and imagine how that activity will be performed.

Step 3

Ask:

- Who is going to perform the activity?
- Will they require special skills or knowledge?

Make a list, in column 2, of the numbers and skills of all the human resources required.

Example

If the project requires building activities, it must be decided whether a building contractor or individuals are going to be employed to do the work. If a contractor, then this information would be entered on the form.

If, however, it is decided to employ group members to do the work, an estimate must be made of the number and skills required. The information is then entered on the form.

While making out a list of human resources, the need for training (not listed on the original project plan) might be identified. This could be added on to the plan and the project resources form.

ACTIVITIES	Qty	HUMAN	Qty	EQUIPMENT	Qty	MATERIALS
		RESOURCES				
Construction of storage bond	1	Contract with Building Contractor				

ACTIVITIES	Qty	HUMAN	Qty	EQUIPMENT	Qty	MATERIALS
		RESOURCES				
Construction of storage bond	2	Carpenters				
	1	Electrician				
	3	Labourers				

ACTIVITIES	Qty	HUMAN	Qty	EQUIPMENT	Qty	MATERIALS
		RESOURCES				
Construction of storage bond	2	Carpenters				
	1	Electrician				
	3	Labourers				
Training of Group Members in general building skills	1	Building Instructor				

All project activities should be examined and the human resources requirements identified.

Step 4

For each activity, decide if equipment will be required. The equipment might be bought, rented or borrowed. Enter the information in column 3 of the form.

Example

A village farming group is going to increase the size of their farms. This will require clearing 10 acres of forest. The information is entered on the form as shown.

ACTIVITIES	Qty	HUMAN	Qty	EQUIPMENT	Qty	MATERIALS
		RESOURCES				
Clear forest for 10 acre farm	1	Power Saw Operator	1	Rented Power Saw		
	3	Helpers	2	Axes		
			4	Cutlass		

All the project activities should be examined and all the equipment required identified.

Step 5

Examine the activities and decide what materials will be required. Enter the information in column 4 of the form.

Example

A group is redecorating their Community Hall kitchen. One of the activities will be the painting of the kitchen. The materials required are entered on the form.

ACTIVITIES	RESOURCES					
	Qty	HUMAN	Qty	EQUIPMENT	Qty	MATERIALS
Painting of Community Centre kitchen	1	Painter			5g	Under coat paint
	1	Helper			8g	White gloss paint
					2	2" paint brush
					1	1" paint brush

> **Do not forget transportation costs**

It is very likely that the equipment and materials will have to be transported. Also, members of the group committee will have to travel to the bank or attend meetings. Transportation costs can be high, so allowance should be made when compiling a cost estimate for a project.

When preparing a project cost estimate, consideration should be given to whether the following transportation costs will occur:

- Delivering equipment and materials.
- Journeys by group members to attend meetings, visit the bank, make purchases etc.
- Visits by non-group members to perform tasks on behalf of the group.

A transportation requirement form can be drawn up and used to identify all the transportation requirements. The form should be completed at the same time as the project resources form.

Examples of possible journeys and their entry on the form are shown in the illustration opposite.

Cost estimating

With the aid of the project resources and the transportation requirements forms, the project resource requirements can be identified. It is necessary to decide how these requirements can be satisfied. The project resources form should be examined and a

DESCRIPTION	JOURNEY DETAILS			
	No.	From	To	Cost $
Monthly visit by the Treasurer to the Bank	18	Afford	Rentown	3,500
Quarterly meeting with Funding Agency, attended by 3 Committee members	5	Afford	Georgetown	32,250
Visit of Chairman and one Committee member to Georgetown to obtain prices for equipment.	1	Afford	Georgetown	4,300
Hire of tractor and trailer to collect wood.	1	Afford	Rentown	11,000
Transporting chain saw purchased in Georgetown	1	Georgetown	Afford	3,250
etc				

list made of all the skills and labour requirements. Members of the group should be consulted to determine whether they or people from the community can do the work, or whether a contractor will have to be employed. A list can then be made of the group and community members who can take an active part in the project.

Most projects will require financial expenditure. A project cost estimate will have to be prepared to determine the amount of money required to finance the project. This can be done as follows.

In Chapter 3, it was shown how projects are easier to plan and manage if they are organized into smaller 'part' projects. Similarly, in preparing cost estimates it helps if the activities are grouped into the same part projects.

Example

For an overall project to build a Crafts Training Centre, the 'part' projects could be:

- Acquiring the land
- Designing the building
- Installing the foundations
- Building the walls etc.

During the planning of a project, the activities of each of the part projects should be identified. Using the procedures described above, the resources required can be identified. A cost estimate for each of those resources must be calculated.

With prices increasing continuously, how can future costs be estimated? When preparing estimates, the current costs must be used. It will be shown later how a contingency factor is used to allow for possible increases in costs.

> When preparing estimates, use known current costs:
> do not guess what future costs might be

Expenditure can be grouped under **five** headings and their costs determined as follows.

LABOUR COSTS

These can arise due to the work performed by individuals employed by the group, or by a contractor. In the case of labour employed directly by the group these have been identified and listed on the project resources form. To estimate the cost requires the number of man days for each group of skills (carpenters, helpers, farmers etc) to be multiplied by the unit cost.

Example

Three carpenters are required to work for five days to build a secure building for storage (locally known as a 'storage bond'). They are each paid $500 per day.

The total number of carpenter days is 3 x 5 = 15 man days

The total cost for the carpenters is 15 x $500 = $7,500

To assist in the preparation of estimates, a simple form can be drawn up and completed.

When a group has to employ a contractor to perform work, a cost quotation should be obtained. To do this, a description will have to be given to the contractor of the work to be done, and a written esti-

"PART" PROJECT: CONSTRUCTION OF STORAGE BOND

DETAILS	SKILL	MAN DAYS	COST PER MAN DAY	TOTAL COST
Constructing walls and frame for roof	CARPENTER (3)	3 x 5 =15	500	7500
Installing roof	CARPENTER (1)	1	500	500
etc				300
	HELPER (1)	1	300	
			TOTAL	8300

mate of the cost of performing the work must be supplied by the contractor. The quotation of costs should state exactly what work the contractor will do and what materials and equipment the contractor will provide. Procedures for obtaining quotations are described in more detail in Chapter 8. Some contractors might require a fee to be paid for providing a quotation.

MATERIALS

A list of all the required materials can be made from the information detailed on the project resources form. These can be grouped together according to the likely suppliers. Estimates can then be obtained from suppliers for the cost of the materials.

To assist in the preparation of the estimates, a simple form can be drawn up and completed.

"PART" PROJECT: CONSTRUCTION OF STORAGE BOND			
NAME OF SUPPLIER: ACE SUPPLIES Ltd. Rentown.			
DESCRIPTION	Quantity	Unit Cost	COST
Soft wood 3" x 3" ,, 12" x 1"	100 BM 50 BM	$30/BM ,,	3000 1500
2" Nails	2 lbs	$20/lb	40
etc.			
		TOTAL	$ 4540

EQUIPMENT

A list of all the equipment can be made from the information detailed on the project resources form. Equipment requirements can be grouped together according to likely suppliers. Estimates can then be obtained from suppliers for the costs of either buying or renting the equipment.

"PART" PROJECT: COMMUNITY FARM PROJECT, LAND CLEARANCE			
NAME OF SUPPLIER: MAIN TRADING Co. Ltd., Georgetown			
DESCRIPTION	Quantity	Unit Cost	COST
STHIL # 70 Chain Saw	1	$180,000	180,000
Cutlass	20	400	8000
etc.			
		TOTAL	$ 188,000

TRANSPORTATION AND ACCOMMODATION

By using a transportation requirement form, the transportation costs likely to be incurred during the project can be estimated. When attending meetings or paying visits to purchase materials, it might not be possible to complete these activities in a day, and an overnight stay will be required. Therefore, in addition to the transportation costs, consideration should be given to whether an allowance has to be made for accommodation.

MISCELLANEOUS

Expenditure can occur which cannot be grouped with any of the other items. For example, the group might seek the assistance of an external organization to help with training. Or the group might have to pay rent for the use of a building or land. These costs could be identified under miscellaneous.

To obtain the estimated total cost of the project, the costs of each of the part projects have to be totalled up and added together, as in the following example.

Example

A group of farmers come together to organize a project which consists of:

- *Clearing 50 acres of riverside land.*
- *Digging a main drainage trench and ditches.*
- *Planting the land, and tending the crops.*
- *Building a secure storage building.*
- *Buying and distributing tools and chemicals to the group members.*
- *Buying a boat and outboard engine (to transport farm products to market).*

"PART" PROJECT	ESTIMATE OF COSTS					
	LABOUR	MATER'S	EQUIP'	TRANSP'	MISCEL '	TOTAL
Land clearance	100,000	10,000	200,000	20,000	-	330,000
Drainage scheme	575,000	50,000	250,000	25,000	-	900,000
Planting crops etc.	30,000	20,000	-	5,000	-	55,000
Storage bond	20,000	30,000	-	5,000	10,000	65,000
Tools and chemicals	-	50,000	50,000	5,000	-	105,000
Boat and Engine	-	-	500,000	45,000	-	545,000
TOTAL	725,000	160,000	1,000,000	105,000	10,000	2,000,000

The form provides a picture of the required expenditures. It can be seen in the example that the figures in the far right hand column represent the totals for each of the part projects, while the bottom right hand figure is the total project cost ($2,000,000). The bottom row gives the totals for each item, that is, for labour $725,000; for materials $160,000; and so on. Adding the figures along the bottom row also gives the estimated total project cost.

For a simple project, there would be no need to divide the project into part projects. The above project cost estimate summary form can be used to detail the estimates for each of the project activities.

Allowance must be made for one other expenditure item, namely **administration**. This includes the costs of postage, telephone calls, stationery, holding meetings etc. A simple way of treating these costs is to make an allowance based on a percentage of the total estimated project cost, normally 5%. So, for the farming project detailed above, an allowance of 5% of $2,000,000, i.e $100,000.

It is very difficult to estimate the **precise cost** of a project. Not all activities might have been identified during the planning stage. Also during the life of the project circumstances could change, resulting in additional expenditure. Even when all the items of expenditure have been correctly identified, costs

"PART" PROJECT	ESTIMATE OF COSTS					
	LABOUR	MATER'S	EQUIP'	TRANSP'	MISCEL '	TOTAL
Land clearance	100,000	10,000	200,000	20,000	-	330,000
Drainage scheme	575,000	50,000	250,000	25,000	-	900,000
Planting crops etc.	30,000	20,000	-	5,000	-	55,000
Storage bond	20,000	30,000	-	5,000	10,000	65,000
Tools and chemicals	-	50,000	50,000	5,000	-	105,000
Boat and Engine	-	-	500,000	45,000	-	545,000
SUB TOTAL	725,000	160,000	1,000,000	105,000	10,000	2,000,000
ADMINISTRATION @ 5% of estimated project cost						100,000
TOTAL ESTIMATED PROJECT COST						2,100,000

can increase due to inflation. Therefore allowance must be made to cover these possibilities. A **contingency** item is added to the estimate. This is calculated as a percentage of the total project cost, and can vary between 5% to 25% depending on the confidence in the accuracy of the project estimate and the rate of inflation. If the estimate is thought to be accurate and the rate of inflation is low, then a contingency of 5% can be used. However, for high risk projects or if the current rate of inflation is high, an allowance of 25% should be made. It could be thought wise to always use 25%. However, if you use too high a figure, it could make the cost of the project appear to be so high that the project is never started. Similarly, there is a danger in selecting too low a contingency figure. If things go wrong you could run out of money before the project is finished.

> Always choose a realistic contingency figure:
> too high a figure and the project might not start;
> too low a figure and the project might never be finished

In the case of the above farming project, there was some doubt over how much drainage would be required. The current rate of inflation was 10%. Therefore it was decided that a contingency figure based on 15% should be used, giving a final project cost estimate of $2,415,000.

"PART" PROJECT	ESTIMATE OF COSTS					
	LABOUR	MATER'S	EQUIP'T	TRANS'	MISCEL '	TOTAL
Land clearance	100,000	10,000	200,000	20,000	-	330,000
Drainage scheme	575,000	50,000	250,000	25,000	-	900,000
Planting crops etc.	30,000	20,000	-	5,000	-	55,000
Storage bond	20,000	30,000	-	5,000	10,000	65,000
Tools and chemicals	-	50,000	50,000	5,000	-	105,000
Boat and Engine	-	-	500,000	45,000	-	545,000
SUB TOTAL	725,000	160,000	1,000,000	105,000	10,000	2,000,000
ADMINISTRATION @ 5% of estimated project cost						100,000
TOTAL ESTIMATED PROJECT COST						2,100,000
CONTINGENCY @ 15%						315,000
TOTAL ESTIMATED PROJECT EXPENDITURE						2,415,000

Cost estimates are not calculated just to find out the total cost of the project. Chapter 8 will show how the project budget, together with the project plan, are used as important tools to assist in the successful management of projects.

Project cost estimates and plans are useful management tools

It is unlikely that all the project funds will be required at the start of project. For example, in the farming project described above, land clearance must be completed before work can start on the drainage scheme. Similarly, the drainage scheme must be completed before planting of crops can commence. So the expenditure of funds is spread over the period of the project programme.

Using the project plan to identify when actions will take place and the estimates to see the cost of each activity, the expenditure can be 'phased' (spread out) over the project. A project expenditure phasing form can be used to assist. In the case of the farming project it is planned that the project would take 12 months, with most of the activities occurring in the first nine months.

It can be seen that the form provides details of the phasing of the total project and also of the individual part projects.

In addition to expenditure, consideration should be given to income received during the planned project programme. Sources of income could be group membership fees, money earned by the project, etc. For example, in the project described above the boat and engine will

"PART" PROJECT or ACTIVITIES	EXPENDITURE PHASING				EXPEN' TOTAL
	1st Quarter	2nd Quarter	3rd Quarter	4th Quarter	
Land clearance	130,000	200,000	-	-	330,000
Drainage Scheme	100,000	300,000	500,000	-	900,000
Planting crops etc	-	-	20,000	35,000	55,000
Storage Bond	-	10,000	55,000	-	65,000
Tools and Chemicals	-	50,000	55,000	-	105,000
Boat and Engine	400,000	145,000	-	-	545,000
Administration	25,000	25,000	25,000	25,000	100,000
SUB TOTAL	655,000	730,000	655,000	60,000	2,100,000
CONTIN' 15%	98,000	110,000	98,000	9,000	315,000
PROJECT TOTAL	753,000	840,000	753,000	69,000	2,415,000

"PART" PROJECT or ACTIVITIES	EXPENDITURE PHASING				EXPENDITURE TOTAL
	1st Quarter	2nd Quarter	3rd Quarter	4th Quarter	
Land clearance	130,000	200,000	-	-	330,000
Drainage Scheme	100,000	300,000	500,000	-	900,000
Planting crops etc	-	-	20,000	35,000	55,000
Storage Bond	-	10,000	55,000	-	65,000
Tools and Chemicals	-	50,000	55,000	-	105,000
Boat and Engine	400,000	145,000	-	-	545,000
Administration	25,000	25,000	25,000	25,000	100,000
SUB TOTAL	655,000	730,000	655,000	60,000	2,100,000
CONTIN' 15%	98,000	110,000	98,000	9,000	315,000
TOTAL Expenditure	753,000	840,000	753,000	69,000	2,415,000
TOTAL INCOME	-	-	(100,000)	(100,000)	(200,000)
TOTAL FUNDS REQUIRED	753,000	840,000	653,000	(31,000)	2,215,000

be purchased during the first two quarters. Therefore after the first six months the boat could be used to carry freight and passengers, so earning income for the project. It is estimated that the boat will earn $100,000 every three months. The form can be modified to show the income and so allow the funds required for the project to be calculated.

It can be seen that the total estimated income is $200,000 and so the funds required to finance the project are reduced to $2,215,000. In the last quarter the income is even greater than the planned expenditure, so the funding for the project will be required in the first three quarters.

Questions and exercises

It is suggested that you read Chapters 3 and 4 before attempting the following exercises and questions.

RESOURCE IDENTIFICATION

Question: Has a project plan been prepared?

Question: Have all the activities necessary for achieving the project objectives been identified?

Question: Which of the group members can help to identify the skills required to perform the project activities?

Exercise: Draw up a project resources form and list in column (1) all the identified project activities.

ACTIVITIES	RESOURCES					
	Qty	HUMAN	Qty	EQUIPMENT	Qty	MATERIALS
(1)		(2)		(3)		(4)

Exercise: Examine the activities and decide which will require human resources.

For each of these activities enter, in column (2) of the project resources form, the type of skills required.

Question: Are there members of the group with the required skills?

Question: Who can provide the necessary skills?

Exercise: Enter in column (2) of the form the names of the individuals or contractor who can perform the work.

Question: Will the group members require training before they can perform the project activities?

Exercise: Enter in column (1) of the project resources form the type of training required.

Exercise: Enter in column (2) the name of the person or organization who can provide the necessary training.

Question: Does the group own any equipment?

Question: Which of the group members can help to identify the equipment required to perform the project activities?

Exercise: Examine the activities and enter in column (3) of the project resources form a list of equipment required.

Question: Can the required equipment be borrowed from group members?

Question:	Need the equipment be purchased or will it be cheaper to rent it?
Exercise:	*Enter in column (3) of the project resources form where the equipment will be obtained, and whether it will be rented, borrowed or bought.*
Question:	Who is going to operate the equipment?
Exercise:	*Enter the names in column (2) of the form.*
Question:	Will the operators require training? Who can provide the training?
Question:	Does the group own any materials?
Question:	Which of the group members can help to identify the materials required to perform the project activities?
Exercise:	*Examine the activities and enter in column (4) of the project resources form a list of materials required.*
	Enter in column (4) of the project resources form where the materials can be obtained.
Question:	How will the group find out the price of materials and equipment?
Question:	Who will be going to buy the materials and equipment?
Question:	Will transportation be required to deliver the equipment and materials to the project site?
Question:	Will representatives of the group have to make journeys to attend meetings, or to make regular visits to the bank?

DESCRIPTION	JOURNEY DETAILS			
	No.	From	To	Cost

Exercise:	*Examine the information recorded on the project resources form, and identify what and how many journeys group members will have to make.*
Question:	Will overnight stays be required?
Exercise:	*Enter the answers on the transportation requirements form.*
Exercise:	*Identify and record on the transportation requirements form materials and equipment transportation requirements.*

COST ESTIMATING

Question: When preparing cost estimates, should current costs or estimated future costs be used?

Question: How is allowance made for possible increases in costs?

Question: When planning the project, were the activities grouped into 'part'
projects?

Question: Will it be helpful when preparing cost estimates to group activities into part projects?

Labour costs

Question: Are there group members who can assist in estimating labour
costs?

Exercise: *For each of the part projects, examine the project resources form
and list, in columns (1) and (2) of the labour costs estimating
form, details of the activities and skill requirements.*

Exercise: *Examine each activity listed in column
(1) of the labour
costs estimating
form and the project
plan, and estimate
for each skill how
long each activity
will take. Enter the
answers in column (3).*

"PART" PROJECT:				
DETAILS	SKILL	MAN DAYS	COST PER MAN DAY	TOTAL COST
			TOTAL	

Exercise: *For each skill, enter in column (4) of the form the cost per man
day (or hour).*

*For each activity calculate the cost for each skill, and enter the
answers in column (5).*

Question: Will a contractor have to be employed to undertake some of the
project activities?

Question: What project activities will be performed by a contractor?

Question: Are there group members who can assist in identifying a suitable
contractor?

> Take great care when selecting a contractor

Question: What is a 'work specification'?

Question: Are there group members who can assist in writing a description of the work to be performed by a contractor?

Question: What details should be included in a work specification?

Question: Will the contractor be responsible for providing all tools, equipment, materials, labour and transportation?

Question: Is it satisfactory for a contractor to tell you the price he will charge for doing the work, or should a written quotation be obtained?

Question: What details should a contractor include in the written quotation?

Question: Should an estimate be obtained from only one contractor, or should a second quotation be obtained in order to make a comparison?

Question: If quotations are obtained from more than one contractor, how should the group decide which contractor to employ?

Question: Should the contractor submitting the lowest estimate always be employed?

Question: Other than cost, what other factors should be considered when choosing a contractor?

Exercise: *Enter details of the quotation of the chosen contractor on the labour costs estimating form.*

Question: What is the total labour cost for each of the part projects?

Materials costs

Question: Are there group members who can assist in identifying suitable suppliers of materials?

Exercise: *For each of the part projects, examine the project resources form and list, in columns (1) and (2) of the materials costs estimating form, details of the materials and quantities required.*

"PART" PROJECT:			
NAME OF SUPPLIER:			
DESCRIPTION	Quantity	Unit Cost	COST
		TOTAL	

Question: What factors should be considered when choosing suppliers?

Question: Should estimates of costs be obtained from more than one supplier?

Exercise: *Enter the price quotations received from the chosen supplier in columns (3) and (4) of the materials costs estimating form.*

Question: What is the total value of the materials required for each of the part projects?

Equipment costs

Question: Are there group members who can assist in identifying suitable suppliers of rented equipment?

Question: Is the equipment required for the project going to be purchased or rented?

Exercise: *Enter in columns (1) and (2) of the equipment costs estimating form the details and the quantity of the equipment to be rented.*

Question: What factors should be considered when choosing suppliers?

Question: Should estimates of costs be obtained from more than one supplier?

Exercise: *Enter the price quotations received from the chosen supplier in columns (3) and (4) of the equipment costs estimating form.*

"PART" PROJECT:				
NAME OF SUPPLIER:				
DESCRIPTION		Quantity	Unit Cost	COST
		TOTAL		

Question: What is the total cost of *renting* equipment for each part project?

Question: Are there group members who can assist in identifying suitable suppliers to purchase equipment from?

Exercise: *Enter in columns (1) and (2) of a new equipment costs estimating form details and the quantity of the equipment to be purchased.*

Question: What factors should be considered when choosing suppliers?

Question: Should estimates of costs be obtained from more than one supplier?

Exercise: *Enter the price quotations received from the chosen supplier in columns (3) and (4) of the equipment costs estimating form.*

Question: What is the total cost of purchasing equipment for each part project?

Transportation and accommodation costs

Question: Have all the journeys to be made by group members to attend meetings and visit the bank been identified on the transportation requirements form?

DESCRIPTION	JOURNEY DETAILS			
	No.	From	To	Cost

Question: Have all the journeys required to deliver equipment and materials been identified on the transportation requirements form?

Question: During the planned visits, will the group representatives have to make overnight stays? Have all these been identified on the transportation requirements form?

Question: What is the total cost of transportation and accommodation for each part project?

Miscellaneous costs

Question: Will the group require the assistance of external organizations to provide training? What will be the costs?

Question: Will the group have to pay rent for the use of buildings or land?

Question: What other identified project costs have not been listed on the cost estimating forms?

Question: What are the total miscellaneous costs for each of the part projects?

Total project costs

Exercise: List all the part projects (or for small projects, their activities) in column (1) of the project cost estimate summary form. Using the information detailed on the completed cost estimating forms, for each part project (or

"PART" PROJECT	ESTIMATE OF COSTS					
	LABOUR	MATER'S	EQUIP'T	TRANS'	MISCEL'	TOTAL
SUB TOTAL						
ADMINISTRATION @ 5 % of estimated project cost						
TOTAL ESTIMATED PROJECT COST						
CONTINGENCY @ %						
TOTAL ESTIMATED PROJECT EXPENDITURE						

*for small projects, their activities), enter on the project cost estimate form, the estimated costs for: **Labour, Materials, Equipment, Transportation** and **Miscellaneous.***

Question: What are the sub-totals for **Labour, Materials, Equipment, Transportation** and **Miscellaneous?**

Question: What is the total when all the values in the sub-totals row are added together?

Question: What is the total when all the part project total costs are added together?

Administration costs

Question: What are the administration costs of a project?

Question: What simple way can be used to estimate administration costs of a project?

Question: What is 5% of the total cost of the part projects?
(i.e. multiply the total cost by 0.05).

Exercise: *Enter the calculated administration cost on the project cost estimate summary form.*

Contingency allowance

Question: Why is it necessary to add a contingency allowance to the project estimate?

Question: How is the project contingency figure estimated?

Question: What factors should be considered when deciding on the percentage of the total estimated project cost to be used as the project contingency figure?

Question: What is the current rate of inflation?

Question: How much confidence is there that *all* the project activities have been identified?

Question: Are there any risks of the project not going according to the plan?

Question: What percentage should be used to calculate the project contingency figure?

Exercise: *Enter the calculated contingency percentage and figure on the project cost estimate summary form.*

Question: What is the total estimated project expenditure?

Expenditure phasing

Question: What is meant by 'expenditure phasing'?

Question: Will the group require all the funds at the start of the project?

Question: Will all the part projects occur at the same time?

Question: Will some part projects be completed before others begin?

"PART" PROJECT or ACTIVITIES	EXPENDITURE PHASING				EXPENDITURE TOTAL
	1st Quarter	2nd Quarter	3rd Quarter	4th Quarter	
SUB TOTAL					
CONTIN' %					
TOTAL Expenditure					
TOTAL INCOME					
TOTAL FUNDS REQUIRED					

Exercise: List the part projects in column (1) of the project expenditure phasing form.

Using the **project plan** and the **project expenditure estimate**, determine the timing and the amount of funds required throughout the project. (It will be easier to work out the phasing, if the project is divided up into four periods of equal length. For example, if the project is due to last 16 months, each period would be four months long.)

Enter the answers on the project expenditure phasing form.

Question: What are the sub-total expenditures for each quarter?

Exercise: Multiply each sub-total by the percentage chosen for the project contingency. For example, if 15% contingency is used multiply by 0.15, or if 10% contingency is used multiply by 0.1, or for 5% multiply by 0.05.

Enter the calculated contingency for each quarter on the project expenditure phasing form.

Question: What is the total project expenditure for each quarter?

Question: What is the total estimated project expenditure of the group's project?

Question: Is the figure of the total estimated project expenditure calculated on the project expenditure phasing form the same as that calculated on the project cost estimate summary form?

Income earning projects

Question: Will the group's project be earning income during the planned project programme? If the answer is yes, when will it start earning income, and how much will it earn each quarter?

Exercise: *If the answer to the above question is yes, enter the estimated income figures for each quarter on the project expenditure phasing form.*

Question: What will be the total funds required by the group for the project?

Question: How much funding will the group require each quarter?

Check that the estimate is correct

The following seven forms can be used or adapted for the group's own resource identification and cost estimating.

PROJECT RESOURCES FORM

ACTIVITIES	RESOURCES					
	Qty	HUMAN	Qty	EQUIPMENT	Qty	MATERIALS

TRANSPORTATION REQUIREMENTS FORM

| DESCRIPTION | JOURNEY DETAILS | | | |
	No.	From	To	Cost

TOTAL COST $

LABOUR COSTS ESTIMATING FORM

'PART' PROJECT:-

DETAILS	SKILL	MAN DAYS	COST PER MAN DAY	TOTAL COST
			TOTAL $	

MATERIALS/EQUIPMENT COSTS ESTIMATING FORM

'PART' PROJECT			
NAME OF SUPPLIER:-			
DESCRIPTION	Quantity	Unit Cost	COST $
			TOTAL $

MISCELLANEOUS COSTS ESTIMATING FORM

'PART' PROJECT:-

DESCRIPTION	SUPPLIER	COST $
		TOTAL $

PROJECT COST ESTIMATE SUMMARY FORM

'PART' PROJECT or ACTIVITY	ESTIMATE OF COSTS						
	LABOUR	MATERIALS	EQUIPMENT	TRANSP'	MISCEL'	TOTAL	
Sub Total							

ADMINISTRATION @ 5% of estimated project cost.

TOTAL ESTIMATED PROJECT COST

CONTINGENCY @   %

TOTAL ESTIMATED PROJECT EXPENDITURE

PROJECT EXPENDITURE PHASING FORM

| 'PART' PROJECT or ACTIVITIES | EXPENDITURE | | | | EXPENDITURE TOTAL |
	1st Quarter	2nd Quarter	3rd Quarter	4th Quarter	$
SUB TOTAL					
CONTINGENCY %					
TOTAL EXPENDITURE					
TOTAL INCOME					
TOTAL FUNDS REQUIRED					

CHAPTER 5
Project funding

Most projects will require some financial expenditure. Chapter 4 described how to identify the resources required and estimate costs.

A decision will have to be made on how to finance a project. There are three possible sources of funds:

- Self help
- Loans
- Grants

Self help

There are many forms of self help. Each has in common that the group provides all or part of the necessary funds or resources. These can be obtained by:

- The group organizing fund-raising events, raffles, shows, barbecues, etc.
- If the group owns equipment, goods or property that it no longer wants, these can be sold to obtain funds.
- Group members can make gifts to the group of money, and items that could be used for the project or sold to raise funds.
- If the group participates in commercial enterprises, profits from these can be used to finance the new project.
- Group members can give their time to perform project tasks unpaid.

Loans

A loan is money borrowed for an agreed period of time. It costs money to get a loan. The lender charges for the use of the money. Normally, interest is charged at a given percentage rate of the total amount borrowed. So by the end of the agreed loan period, the original amount borrowed plus the interest charged must be paid back.

Example

$100 is borrowed for one year at an annual interest rate of 5%. By the end of the year, the original $100, plus the 5% interest charged, that is (5/100 x $100 = $5) must be paid back, making a total of $100 + $5 = $105

Because the initial amount borrowed plus interest has to be paid back, a loan is only appropriate when the project will make enough money to repay the debt. Suitable projects could be farming, manufacturing, craft businesses and transportation, etc.

Loans for projects such as a community centre or village hall might be suitable, if enough profits can be made from events to cover both the repayments and the ongoing costs of operating the project.

Loans are unsuitable for projects where it is unlikely that they could make enough money to pay off the debt, such as improving roads, building schools etc.

> **Loans are only suitable for projects that can make enough money to pay back the original amount borrowed plus the interest charges**

There are three main sources of loans, as follows.

Private individuals or organizations

Group or community members might be prepared to provide loans. Similarly, organizations or businesses which do not provide loans as their normal business activity might, if they have a close association with the community, be prepared to assist the group by providing a loan.

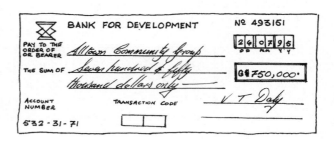

Before entering into such an arrangement both the group and the lender should agree on the terms of the loan: that is, the length of the loan period, the interest to be charged, what would happen if the group fails to make a repayment, and so on. Depending on the relationship between the lender and the group, a legal contract might have to be entered into.

Banks

Banks are in business to make a profit. They do this by charging interest on the money they lend. Banks do not like taking risks. So, to safeguard their money they require borrowers to provide collateral. That is, the borrower must provide some form of security, so that if the borrower fails to pay back the loan and interest, the bank can get back its money by some other means.

Example

A group wants to start up a craft business. They require funds to build a craft centre. The bank could give the loan on condition that the bank holds the deeds (title documents) of the centre. If the group fails to pay back the loan, the bank has the right to sell the centre in order to get back its money.

Banks normally prefer to give loans to existing organizations who have proven their credit worthiness. New groups and businesses might find it more difficult to obtain a bank loan.

If a group considers that its proposed project is suitable for funding by means of a bank loan, the group will have to prepare a 'loan proposal document'. This must show that the group can in the given time make enough profit to pay back the loan and the interest charged.

> **Banks do not like taking risks: a group must provide confidence to the bank that its money would not be at risk**

Banks usually conduct transactions with professionally managed businesses. Therefore, when dealing with banks, groups must demonstrate that they are equally competent.

When preparing a loan proposal document, the information provided must be correct. Also the document should be neat and well presented, if possible typed.

The proposal should include the following information:

- *Description of the group* applying for the loan. Give a brief history of the group. Detail the achievements of the group. Supply information on the number of group members and the names of the executive officers and committee members.
- *Financial support information.* Not only must an itemized budget be provided, but also a business plan. This should give a complete and detailed picture of the income-earning capabilities of the project, i.e. the estimated operating costs, the expected sales, a cash flow budget etc. This must show that the project will make enough money not only to cover the operating costs but also provide sufficient funds to repay the loan and interest charges.

- *Loan requirement*. This should give the exact amount of the funds required and how the money will be spent.
- *Collateral (security)*. What security can the group provide for the loan? Remember banks do not like taking risks, therefore the collateral provided must be of equal or more value than the loan.
- *Business review*. No business or group can operate in isolation. A business is likely to have competitors. The group will have to sell a product or provide a service to obtain funds. To enable the bank to make a decision on whether to provide a loan, it will need information on the overall 'market' in which the enterprise will be operating. The group will have to prove they know what they are doing and are competent.

After preparing the loan proposal document, the group can make contact with a bank. A letter should be written to the bank manager requesting an appointment to discuss the loan application. No bank will grant a loan without first meeting the applicants. The main objective of the letter is to obtain a meeting. Consequently, the letter should only contain a brief description of the group and the proposed project. Full details should be provided at the meeting.

Enterprise development agencies

Due to the difficulties new groups and small businesses have in obtaining loans, enterprise development agencies have been formed to assist such groups to start new businesses. While it might be easier to obtain a loan from such agencies, they have rules governing their operations. Typically, some of these could be:

- The loans are only given to non-government organizations (NGOs). This means that while community development groups can apply, community councils are ineligible.
- The group must have five members who are already in business. There must not be more than one direct family member in each group.
- A group leader is elected to transact business with the agency.
- The same amount is loaned to each member of the group. There is a maximum limit on the first loan given. When the loan is paid back on time, the next loan granted to the group could be up to 50% more and the following one up to another 50% more.
- No collateral is required. Each member guarantees the loans for every other member. This is a very important rule and its consequences must be understood by all the members before an agreement is signed. Simply, it means, **if one or more members fail to pay back the loan, then the other members of the group must pay back that share of the loan as well as their own**.

- Members must make weekly payments into an emergency fund which is held for them by the agency.
- Loans are disbursed (handed) to the individual members of the group. Interest is charged on a fixed weekly rate on the declining balance. Loans must be repaid on time. If the repayments are not made on time, interest will be calculated at a higher rate.
- The group leader is responsible for collecting the repayment instalments and making the payments to the agency. No part payments are allowed.

If members of a group consider that they might qualify for a loan from an enterprise development agency, they should write to or telephone the agency requesting a meeting in order to obtain more information about the schemes. As part of the services provided by the agency, it will often assist in preparing a business plan and budget, together with other training. However, before making contact, group members should first decide on their own objectives and perform an initial review of their proposed business requirements.

Grants

Grants, unlike loans, do not have to be repaid. They are given to finance specific project requirements. The money must not be used by the group to fund activities which were not approved by the agency which gave the grant.

Example

No part of a grant given for the construction of a community centre should be used to give private loans to group members. However, a specific grant could be applied for by a group to enable it to provide loans to its members for stated activities; for example, to permit them to buy tools for their farms.

Similarly, a group which has received funds to provide loans to its members to improve their businesses cannot decide to spend it for other purposes; for example, to use the money to buy a minibus for the group.

Grants are normally given to groups and not to individuals. Some funding agencies will only give grants to non-government organizations (NGOs), and so community or village councils could not obtain a grant from them.

Funding agencies often direct their activities towards target groups. For example, an agency might limit its activities to funding women's projects. Others might concentrate on agricultural projects. For that reason, it is important when seeking a source of funds to find out which organizations provide grants for the type of project the group is proposing. Some agencies run funding programmes for a given period, then might change their target group for the next batch of grants. So it is wise to obtain first-hand information from the agencies, not only about their current aid programme, but also on their future intentions.

The three main sources of grants are:

- *Local individuals or organizations*: grants could be provided by members of a group, friends, local businesses, regional and community councils, religious and other organizations.
- *National organizations*: aid may be provided by big businesses or foundations and organizations established to provide grants for specific or general target groups.
- *International organizations*: development grants may be given by foreign governments or international aid agencies.

In the case of local and national businesses, they might not provide funds, but could give products which can be used in the project or sold to raise funds.

How can a group identify the right agency? An ancient Chinese proverb states that a journey of a thousand miles starts with one first step. So it is with finding funds for a project!

The first step could be:

- To ask the Executive Officer of the region for information on agencies or foundations which have offices in the region. Also ask about agencies which have previously aided groups in the region.
- Look in the local newspapers. Often reports are given on the activities of funding agencies.
- If there are other community groups which have obtained grants, seek information from them.
- Make direct contact with foreign embassies, and the United Nations Development Programme (UNDP), to ask if they or an agency acting on their behalf provide grants. A list of embassies and international agencies with their addresses can be found in the telephone directory.

Even if the organizations contacted cannot assist directly, they will very likely provide information to enable other possible sources of funds to be identified. Once one or more agencies which might provide a grant has been identified, an application can be made. There is no harm in applying to more than one agency. But if this is done, and an agency asks if an application has been made to any other funding source, tell the truth. A lie might damage the relationship with the agency and so hurt the project in the long term.

Even before looking for a donor agency, the group should start to prepare a project proposal document. This is required to provide all the information necessary to convince an agency to approve a grant for the group project. Remember that while the group members are intimately involved with the project and are absolutely convinced of the justification of their case, the person(s) who will decide whether to provide the group with a grant, might have no local knowledge or experience of the problem to be solved. Consequently, great care must be taken in the preparation of the proposal. It should not only provide accurate information, but also give a picture of the problem to be solved and the benefits to be gained as a result of the project.

Some agencies have their own application forms, generally all require the same information. A project proposal document is not only useful when making initial contact with an agency, but if necessary, the information contained can readily be transferred onto an application form.

The following format can be used for a proposal document.

Title. This should highlight the most important feature of the project.

Example

'Reinstatement of a mains water supply to Afford village'.

Summary. A **brief** description of the problem the group is trying to solve; the project; who will benefit from the project and how; the total cost of the project and how much of this the group is applying to the agency for.

Example

Since 1985, the mains water supply to Afford village has failed to operate. It is proposed to replace the unserviceable pump at the well and to install a new water distribution system to all the houses. All 678 residents of the village will benefit. The total estimated cost of the project is $2.5 million, of which $0.5 million will be provided by self help. The balance is the subject of this application.

Introduction. This should give background information on the project. A **brief** description of:

- the community, and how people are affected by the problem to be solved
- the history of the group
- who is going to manage the project
- the main features of the project
- who will benefit from the project and how.

Problem. Describe the problem(s) to be solved by the project. Give full information of how people are affected and where possible how many.

Example

In 1954 a water supply well was drilled at Afford and a windmill driven pump installed. From the mid 1970s there were numerous breakdowns of the windmill and the pump. In 1985 the pump again broke down. Unfortunately, the manufacturer of the pump had gone out of business and no spare parts were available. Since that date the residents of the village have had to obtain their water from a stream located two miles away. This is done by the women and children fetching the water in buckets. During the dry season the water turns brackish and cannot be used.

Objectives. The results to be obtained by the project should be described.

Example

To install a new windmill-driven pump and water distribution system which will provide, throughout the year, an unlimited supply of clean water to every house in the village.

Project activities. Give full details of all the project activities required to achieve the project objectives. Provide information on the project plan with a timetable of key events. If training activities are part of the project, these should also be detailed.

Sustainability. Describe how the objectives of the project will continue to give benefit after the planned project period. If applicable, detail how the facilities provided will continue to be managed and if required, the method of providing funds for the operating costs.

Implementing group. Give details of the name of the group, including a contact address. The history of the group should be provided, detailing when and why the group was formed. State what are the activities of the group, including, if relevant, information on previously managed projects. State the number of members (number of youths, women and men), the names of the executive officers and committee members. Describe how the group will be organized to ensure that the project is effectively and efficiently managed.

Budget and project funding. Give the total cost of the project. Indicate the phasing of the expenditure (see Chapter 4 for information on phasing). If relevant, provide an estimate of the future ongoing operating costs. Explain what contribution the group will make in cash, in kind and/or services. Detail any funds already obtained or promised by other sources, and if any applications have or are going to be made to other sources.

An application can be made to an agency in one of the following ways:

- If the group is sure that their type of project is funded by the agency, write requesting a meeting to discuss the proposed application, and provide the agency with a copy of the project proposal document.
- If the group is unsure whether the agency will fund their type of project, write a letter containing a brief description of the project, and request either a meeting to discuss a possible application or details of the types of projects they fund and an application form.

"PART" PROJECT or ACTIVITIES	EXPENDITURE PHASING				EXPENDITURE TOTAL
	1st Quarter	2nd Quarter	3rd Quarter	4th Quarter	
Land clearance	130,000	200,000	-	-	330,000
Drainage Scheme	100,000	300,000	500,000	-	900,000
Planting crops etc	-	-	20,000	35,000	55,000
Storage Bond	-	10,000	55,000	-	65,000
Tools and Chemicals	-	50,000	55,000	-	105,000
Boat and Engine	400,000	145,000	-	-	545,000
Administration	25,000	25,000	25,000	25,000	100,000
SUB TOTAL	655,000	730,000	655,000	60,000	2,100,000
CONTIN' 15%	98,000	110,000	98,000	9,000	315,000
TOTAL Expenditure	753,000	840,000	753,000	69,000	2,415,000
TOTAL INCOME	-	-	(100,000)	(100,000)	(200,000)
TOTAL FUNDS REQUIRED	753,000	840,000	653,000	(31,000)	2,215,000

It is likely that following an application, the agency will assign a project officer to the group, and explain the agency's requirements for project management, reporting and keeping financial records.

Combined financing

The types of projects suitable for obtaining loans from banks and enterprise development agencies are limited. Also, as a result of local and international factors there has been a reduction in the amount of funds available for grants to community development groups. Consequently, methods have to be devised to maximize the use of available resources.

Most agencies now expect a group to make a contribution in the form of self help. This can be by the group providing money, materials and/or unpaid labour for project activities.

To make the most of available funds, the group should consider whether all or part of the project could be funded by loans rather than grants.

If profit-making activities are undertaken, a group might consider devising its own 'revolving loan scheme' to finance all or part of the project. Rather than using a grant to finance all the project activities, part of the funds might be sought to establish for group members a scheme similar to that provided by an enterprise development agency.

Example

A farming group wanting to increase the amount of land under cultivation might consider financing the proposed project as follows.

The estimated cost of the project is:

	$	$
Land clearance		200,000
Drainage scheme	800,000	
Planting crops		100,000
Building lock-up	50,000	
Buying tools and chemicals		100,000
Training	50,000	
TOTAL	900,000	400,000

An application could be made for a grant to finance the project as follows:

For the direct expenditure by the group for the drainage scheme, building a lock-up and training: $900,000.

A fund of $400,000 to be used to give loans to individual farmers to cover the costs of land clearance, planting crops and buying tools and chemicals. The farmers could be charged a low rate of interest to cover administration costs and to compensate for inflation. When the first set of farmers have paid back their loans, the money can be used to give other farmers loans so that they can also finance improvements to their farms.

If such a revolving loan scheme is initiated, consideration will have to be given to the rules governing the management of the scheme; for example:

- Will collateral have to be provided when a loan is obtained? Or will group members have to form small groups and stand as guarantors for each other?
- Procedures for applying for a loan.
- Procedures for considering loan applications.
- Actions to be taken in the event a member fails to pay back the loan.

Whichever method the group chooses to fund their project, they must prove to potential providers of funds that they are well organized and capable of successfully completing the project.

The first opportunity they will have of demonstrating this is by preparing and presenting an accurate and comprehensive loan application or project proposal document.

> If at first you do not succeed in obtaining funds for your group's project, try again, and again, until you do succeed

Questions and exercises

The following questions and exercises are designed to help you examine the methods available for obtaining funding for a project.

Question: How much money does the group require to fund the proposed project?

Question: What are the three main sources of project funding?

SELF HELP

Question: What activities can a group organize in order to obtain funds?

Question: Can a group organize a concert or show to raise funds?

Exercise: *Make a list of group and community members who could take part in a fund-raising show.*

Question: Does the group own equipment, goods or property that can be sold to obtain funds?

Exercise: *Make a list of all the unwanted equipment, goods and property the group owns. Estimate how much money could be raised if they were sold.*

Question: Are group members prepared to make gifts of money or goods to the group?

Exercise: *Consider what methods can be used to encourage group members to provide financial assistance to the group.*

Question: What other forms of self help are there?

Exercise: *Make a list of all group members who would be prepared to work unpaid on project activities. Are their skills and talents suitable to undertake project tasks?*

Exercise: *Does the group engage in any profit making activities? How much profit is made each year? Is all or part of the profits available to fund a new project?*

LOANS

Question: What types of projects are suitable for funding, totally or in part, by means of loans?

Question: Has the group previously obtained a loan? From whom? Was the loan paid back in full?

Question: Is the group's proposed project suitable for funding, wholly or partly by loans?

Question: Will the project earn money for the group?

Question: Will sufficient money be earned to cover the ongoing operating costs, plus enough to pay back any money borrowed and interest charged?

Question: Is the project a suitable one to be funded by a loan? For how long would the group require to borrow the money?

Question: What is meant by the term 'collateral'?

Question: What security can the group provide against any loan obtained?

Question: What are the main sources of loans?

Private individuals or organizations

Question: Would the members of the group be prepared to give loans for the project?

Question: Are there other people or businesses in the community who could be persuaded to give loans to the group?

Exercise: *Make a list of the people or businesses who may be persuaded to provide loans to the group.*

Question: If private loans are given, should a formal written contract be entered into between the lender and the group?

Question: What items should be covered in any contract?

Banks

Question: Does the group have an account in any bank?

Question: What is the name and address of the closest bank?

Question: What factors do banks take into consideration when deciding whether to grant a loan?

Question: What is meant by 'credit worthiness'?

Question: Does the group have any debts? Has the group a good record of paying back money it owes?

Question: What information should be contained in a loan proposal document?

Question: Is it better to have a meeting with the bank manager before preparing a loan proposal document?

Question: If representatives of the group have a meeting with a bank manager before they have written a loan proposal document, will they have all the answers to any questions the manager might ask?

Question: What skills and talents will be required to write a loan proposal document?

Exercise: *Make a list of all the group and community members who can assist in preparing a loan proposal document.*

> **If in doubt seek training**

Question: What is a 'business plan'?

Question: What information should be contained in a business plan?

Question: What is meant by 'cash flow budget'?

Exercise: *Estimate for each month of the period the group wishes to have a loan:*

(a) The total monthly expenditure (including all operating costs and repayment instalments of the loan and interest charged).
(b) The total monthly receipts (including all money earned by the group).

Question: What form of business will the group be undertaking? Will the group be selling products or providing a service? Who will be the group's main competitors?

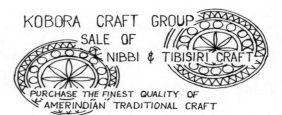

Exercise: *Make a list of the information which will prove that the group is a well managed organization that should be granted a loan.*

Question: What are the weaknesses of the group, which might prevent a loan from being granted? What steps can be taken to strengthen the group's position in these areas? What can be done to compensate for weaknesses?

Exercise:	*Write, in not more than two sentences, a description of the group. Also, in not more than three sentences, give a description of the proposed project.*
Question:	When writing to the bank manager for the first time about a loan, what should be the main objective of the letter?
Exercise:	*Write a letter to a bank manager, requesting a meeting so that you can discuss a loan application.*
Question:	Who are the best persons to represent the group at a meeting with a bank manager?
Question:	Should all the committee members attend, or only a small group who know all the facts and can clearly describe the group's requirements?

Enterprise development agencies

Question:	What are the main differences between a bank and an enterprise development agency?
Question:	Is there an enterprise development agency operating that you can seek funds from?
Question:	What are some of the rules governing the granting of loans by an agency?
Question:	Can the group members be formed into smaller groups in order to stand as guarantors for each other?
Question:	What are the responsibilities of the group members, when they stand as guarantors for each other?
Question:	Are the group's activities suitable for funding by a loan from an enterprise development agency?

GRANTS

Question:	What is the first step a group should take in applying for a loan from an agency?
Question:	What is the main difference between a loan and a grant?
Question:	After obtaining a grant, can a group change its mind and decide to use the funds for some other activity?
Question:	What are the three main sources of grants?
Question:	Are there members of the group or the community who would be prepared to give a grant to the group?

Question:	Are there any large businesses operating in the community who could be persuaded to give a grant?
Question:	How can the group find out the names and addresses of national and international organizations who might give grants?
Question:	Does a member of the group know of any other group who have received a grant?
Exercise:	*Using the section of the telephone directory for the capital city, make a list of all foreign embassies and local aid agencies.*
Question:	Is there any harm in applying to more than one agency for a grant?
Question:	What is the main objective of preparing a project proposal document?
Question:	What information should be contained in a project proposal document?
Question:	What is the title of the group's proposed project?
Question:	What is the problem the group is trying to solve?
Exercise:	*Write a **brief** description of the problem the group is trying to solve and of the project. State who will benefit from the project and how. Indicate the total cost of the project and how much of this the group is applying to the agency for.*
Exercise:	*Write a brief description of the community, and detail how the residents are affected by the problem the group is trying to solve.*
Exercise:	*Describe the main features of the project. What will be the most important activities? Who will perform these activities? Will the group be employing a contractor? Will training be provided to group members?*
Exercise:	*Make a list of the long-term benefits of the project. Will funds be required to ensure that the project continues to provide benefits in the future? Will a committee have to be formed to look after the operation of the project after the initial project period?*
Question:	When was the group formed? How many members are there in the group? Has the group previously undertaken any projects?
Question:	What is the total cost of the project? How much grant money is the group applying for?

102

Exercise: *Write a letter requesting an appointment with an agency to discuss the group's intention to apply for a grant to fund a project. In the letter include a **brief** description of the project.*

COMBINED FINANCING

Question: What factors should be considered when deciding if a project can be funded by means of a combination of loans and grants?

Question: Is the group's proposed project suitable for funding from a number of sources?

Question: What is a 'revolving loan scheme'?

Exercise: *Consider what rules would have to be agreed upon when organizing a revolving loan scheme.*

Exercise: *List the advantages and disadvantages of:*

> *(a) A loan scheme which requires borrowers to provide collateral.*
> *(b) A scheme where a number of members stand as joint guarantors.*

Question: Is it better to require a member who wants a loan to provide collateral, or is the system where another member or members stand as guarantor a better method?

Question: What actions should be taken if a member fails to pay back a loan?

Question: Should a limit be set on the maximum loan a member can receive?

Question: What procedures should be used to decide which members should receive a loan?

> A group should be seen to function
> as a competent organization

CHAPTER 6
Basic bookkeeping and records

Bookkeeping or accounting is keeping a record of details every time money is spent or received.

Most people handle money. They spend it when buying things, and receive it when they sell something or when they are paid wages. Yet, how many people keep a record of these events? Why must a development group keep accounts?

The big difference is that when a person spends his or her own money it is that person's own affair. However, when a group makes a money transaction it is the **group's money** that is being spent. Therefore group members have the right to know what is happening to their money. Also, if a group receives a loan or grant from an aid agency, one of the conditions of obtaining the assistance will be that a record of **all** expenditure must be kept.

It is the responsibility of the group's treasurer to keep a record of all financial transactions. The treasurer must not only show, but also **prove** what has happened to the group's money. The accounts only show how the money has been used; they do not prove how the money has been spent. How can proof be provided? By obtaining and safely keeping all receipts, bills and invoices.

> **Every time money is spent or received proof of the transaction must be obtained**

Invoices and bills

Invoices are given when a credit transaction is undertaken; for example, purchases made or work performed with payment made at a later date. Duplicate invoice books can be purchased. The completed top copy is given to the purchaser while the carbon copy is kept as a record of the transaction. The use of duplicate copies is a simple means of keeping a record of how much money is owed to the group and by whom.

The following is one type of invoice form. When completing an invoice, details must be recorded:

- In the top left hand corner, a reference number. It will be shown later how this number assists when making a check of accounts. The reference number can be either a number or a combination of numbers and letters.

Example

The first invoice could be 001, the next 002, then 003, etc. Or A/001, A/002, A/003.

- Under 'Deliver to:' the name and address of the person or organization making the purchase is entered.
- The date that the transaction takes place.
- Details of the transaction. What was purchased, the quantity and the cost. Or details of the service provided.
- When the goods are delivered, the person who receives them must sign as proof of delivery. The date of delivery must be shown.

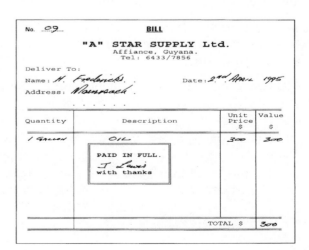

An invoice can also be issued when work is performed, with payment to be made at a later date.

Example

A women's development group decides to build a secure store for their tools and equipment. They know that they will have to wait for the first harvest before they have funds to pay for the work. The contractor agrees to wait for payment for his work. When the construction is finished he issues an invoice for the total cost.

A **bill** is given when a **cash** purchase is made ('cash' can mean payment with money or bank cheque). A bill is also made out when payment is required for a credit transaction. The details recorded are similar to those on an invoice.

When the bill is paid it can be stamped and signed as proof of payment. It then serves as a receipt.

105

Receipts

A **receipt** can be written out and given as proof of **cash payment**. It is important to note that receipts should never be issued for credit, only for cash transactions. Duplicate receipt books can be purchased. After filling in the details, the top page is given to the person making the payment and the carbon copy kept as a record of the transaction.

There are many different designs of receipts but they all allow the following information to be recorded:

- The reference number of the receipt. Each receipt must be given its own number, i.e. the first one 01, the next 02, and so on.

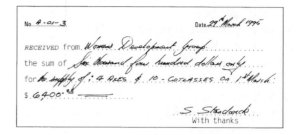

- The date on which payment was received. Receipts must be obtained at the time of payment.
- The full name of the person or organization making the payment.
- The amount paid. This is recorded both in words and at the bottom left hand corner of the receipt in numbers. **'Only' is written after the amount in words, and lines drawn after the amount in figures. This is done to make it more difficult for a dishonest person to change the details**.
- Details of the transaction, i.e. the items purchased or the service provided.

Accounts

Invoices, bills and receipts are the proof of transactions. **Accounts** are kept in order to keep a record of all the **cash** transactions. There are many different ways of recording the information. No single method is better but, whichever one you choose:

- Be consistent. The same rules for recording the information must be used every time.
- The accounts must be 'auditable'. In other words, it must be easy to check that they are correct.

Accounts that can only be understood by the treasurer are of **no use**.

> All members of the group committee should learn to understand the accounts kept. This is important not only to check that the treasurer is keeping correct accounts but also to assist the treasurer to perform his/her duties.

One method of recording **cash** transactions (payment or receipt of either money or a bank cheque) is by keeping a **journal**.

For **every** cash transaction the following information is recorded in the journal:

Column 1   The date of the transaction.

Column 2   Full details of the transaction, i.e. what was purchased or what work was undertaken.

Column 3   The reference number of the bill or receipt or bank cheque.

Column 4   If money is received, the amount in figures is entered. If money is paid out, a short line is drawn through the column to show that no entry has been made.

Column 5   If money is paid out, the amount in figures is entered. If money is received, a short line is drawn through the column to show that no entry has been made.

Date	Details	Ref	Received $	Paid $	Balance $
(1)	(2)	(3)	(4)	(5)	(6)
	BALANCE				

Column 6   The 'balance' records how much money is left after the transaction.

Example

A development group receives a grant of $10,000 from a funding agency on the 1st February 1995.

On the 2nd February the group purchases $2,000 of building materials from 'A' Star Supply Ltd.

On the 3rd February, Marry Williams paid her membership fee of $100, and $600 of nails were purchased from 'Big' Shop.

The page is now full, and no further entries can be made (a journal book can be purchased that will allow far more entries to be made on one page).

Before a new page is started a balance must be made of the first page.

(a) Write down the last balance figure on the bottom line, i.e. $7,500.

(b) Add up all the entries in the received column, and all the entries in the paid column. The two answers are entered on the bottom line.

Date	Details	Ref.	Received $	Paid $	Balance $
1st Feb 95	Funds received from I.D.A. Development Agency.	145	10,000	---	10,000
2nd Feb 95	Purchase of wood from "A" Star Supply Ltd.	A01	------	2,000	8,000
3rd Feb 95	Payment of membership fee by Marry Williams.	001	100	------	8,100
3rd Feb 95	Purchase of nails from 'Big' shop.	B/9	-----	600	7500
3rd Feb 95	BALANCE		10,100	2,600	7,500
			(1)	(2)	(3)

The total received (column 1) is $10,100. The total paid (column 2) is $2,600. If the total of column (2) is subtracted from that of column (1):

$$10,100 - 2,600 = 7,500$$

Note that this is the same as the balance entered in column (3).

> ### The total received, minus the total paid, **must** equal the balance

If the difference does not equal the balance, either a mistake has been made in the calculations, or figure(s) have been entered in wrong column(s).

The advantage of using a journal is that it provides a method to check whether mistakes have been made.

The next transaction should not be waited for before starting the new page. When the page has been balanced correctly, the next page should be started.

This is done as follows:

(a) Enter the page number.

(b) Enter the date in the first column.

(c) Under details write, 'Balance Brought Forward' or, for short, 'Balance B/F'.

(d) Enter the figures from the bottom of the received, paid and balance columns on the previous page onto the top line of the new page.

Date	Details	Ref.	Received $	Paid $	Balance $
3rd Feb 95	Balance Brought Forward		10,100	2,600	7,500
	BALANCE				

108

Project diary

As well as keeping a journal, there are also advantages in keeping a **project diary**. Projects can take months or even several years to complete. During this time there may be changes in the membership of the group committee. By keeping a diary the group will always have a record of the main events that occurred during the project life. This will enable the group members to check back on why decisions were taken and to learn from their mistakes and also from what was done correctly.

It will also provide information to enable the group to make decisions in the future.

Each day, record the date and a **brief** description of the important project events that occurred that day. A school's exercise book can be used for the purpose.

Example

A group managing a community farm project could record:

- *Purchase of planting materials, tools, chemicals, etc.*
  How much was purchased, the supplier's name and the price paid. Additional information could include whether a discount was obtained.
- *The time spent working on the farm. The names of the group members who helped with the work. Were they paid?*
- *What and how much was planted in each field.*
- *The amount of crop harvested from each field.*

*From the above information together with the details recorded in the journal, the **cost** of producing the crop can be calculated. Knowing the cost the group can then decide upon the price they want to charge for their products.*

After the crop is sold, details of the sale should also be recorded in the diary. Soon the group will gather useful information which will help them to make decisions on what crops to plant in the future; for example, will they make more profit from planting cassava or beans?

Bank accounts

Consideration must be given to the safe keeping of the group's funds. If this is only a small amount the committee might decide that the treasurer or some other committee member should keep the money safe. However, if the group receives a loan or a grant, it is likely that the funds will be paid by cheque. For a large amount a bank account should be opened in the name of the group.

> A bank account must be in the name of the group
> **never** in the name of a committee member

There are two types of bank accounts, **deposit** and **current**. Both have their advantages and disadvantages.

Type of account	Advantages	Disadvantages
Deposit	The group's money earns interest	Representatives of the group have to go to the bank to make withdrawals
Current	Funds can be withdrawn by writing a cheque. There is no need to go to the bank to make withdrawals	The account does not earn interest

With a **deposit** account the bank pays interest on the money deposited. If the interest is set at 10%, then the group's money earns $1 for every $10 kept in the account for one year.

Example

If the group places $100 in a deposit account, one year later it would have earned $10, so it would then have $100 + $10 = $110 in the account.

With a **current** account the group is given a cheque book. With cheques, group representatives do not have to go to the bank to make withdrawals. All cheques can be written in the name of the person or organization who is to receive payment. Then they can go to the bank to obtain the money.

A cheque is filled in as follows:

- The day's date is entered in the top right hand corner.
- On the next line, the name of the organization or person who is to receive the money.
- On the two lines below the amount in words.
  Note that the word '**only**' **and two lines** have been drawn in. This is done to prevent anyone from changing the amount of the cheque.

- The amount in figures is entered in the box. Again **two lines** are drawn in, to prevent figures from being added.
- The authorized signatories sign the cheque at the bottom right hand corner.

In the bottom left hand corner there is the number of the account, and the number of the cheque. Like a receipt, each cheque has its own reference number.

If the bank account is in the name of the group, the group will have to nominate who can make payments into and withdrawals from the account. Whether it is a deposit or current account, normally three members of the group committee are selected to be the signatories for the account. Any two of the three can sign a cheque, or for a deposit account go to the bank with the bank book to make a deposit or withdrawal.

A group can open a bank account as follows. After the three persons who will administer the account have been chosen, they should go to the bank taking with them:

- Their National Identification Cards or other appropriate forms of identification.
- A letter of authorization from the group, stating what type of account should be opened and identifying the three persons who will be the signatories.

RECORD KEEPING

As well as keeping safe all bills, invoices, receipts and other financial records, all other group and project documents must be kept safe. These include:

- All agreements and contracts entered into by the group.
- All correspondence, both letters received and those sent by the group. Always make a copy of letters sent.
- Minutes of meetings.

> Always keep safe all records of group activities:
> they will provide information to help the
> group make decisions

Questions and exercises

Irrespective of whether the project is financed by a loan or a grant, or even by means of self help, records will have to be kept of how the group spends its money. The questions and exercises are designed to assist participants to become familiar with the required accounting procedures.

Question: What is meant by the term 'financial transaction'?

Question: What is meant when you 'make a purchase on credit'?

Question: Why should a group keep accounts of its financial transactions?

Question: Does the group or the treasurer have a preferred way of keeping accounts?

Question: How will the group fund its project?

Question: Will the group be receiving a loan or a grant from another organization?
Will they require accounts to be kept?
Has the group discussed with them the method to be used for keeping accounts and how often the funding agency will want to examine them?

INVOICES AND BILLS

Question: What other records and documents, apart from accounts, must be kept?

Question: Why do you have to keep all invoices, bills and receipts?

Question: When is an invoice obtained?

Question: Is the statement 'you do not record **credit** transactions in accounts' correct?

Question: How can a record of credit transactions be kept?

RECEIPTS

Question: Why should a receipt always be obtained when making a purchase for the group?

Question: Is a receipt given to someone buying on credit?

Exercise: *On 1st February, John and his brother Mark Williams pay their group membership fee of $100 each. How many receipts should be written, one or two?*

Write out one of the receipts. Give it the number 01.

No. . . . .   **Date** . . . .

Received from . . . .

the sum of . . . .

for . . . .

$ . . . .

. . . .

With thanks

Question: Will the group members have to pay a membership fee?
Will membership cards or receipts be issued?

Exercise: *100 orange plant seedlings have been sold to the Karria Agricultural Group. They each cost $50. They were delivered on 15th January and paid for on 1st February. Write out the required receipt.*

No. . . . .   **Date** . . . .

Received from . . . .

the sum of . . . .

for . . . .

$ . . . .

. . . .

With thanks

Question: On what date should the receipt have been issued, 15th January or 1st February?
Why?

113

ACCOUNTS

Question: Should the group committee members all learn and understand the methods used for keeping the group's accounts?

Question: What arrangements can be made to train the committee members in accounting procedures?

Question: Should only the committee members be trained, or should all members of the group have the opportunity to be trained?

Question: What is meant by 'accounts must be auditable'?

Question: Who will audit the group's accounts?
How frequently will they be audited?

Question: Why should the reference number of a receipt or bill or cheque be written in the journal for every transaction?

Exercise: *Enter the following details and transactions into **page 2** of the journal:*

- *17th March, Balance Brought Forward, received $10,000, paid $1,000, Balance $9,000.*

- *18th March, received payment of $100 membership fee from George Prince (Receipt number 04).*

- *19th March, purchase of 10 cutlasses at $400 each (Receipt number 97).*

- *25th March, deposit payment of $5,000 for the purchase of an outboard motor (Receipt number A19).*

- *26th March, received loan from bank of $5,000.*

*Make out the balance for the page, and carry the balance forward to **page 3** of the Journal.*

Date	Details	Ref.	Received $	Paid $	Balance $
	BALANCE				

Date	Details	Ref.	Received $	Paid $	Balance $

Question: A group member asks to be given a loan. The borrower promises to pay back the money the next day. Should this transaction be entered in the journal?

Hint First, consideration must be given to whether the group constitution allows loans to be given to members. If it does, rules should be put in place to cover who can approve the loan. It is suggested that the approval of at least two executive members be required.

Even though the repayment is to be made within a short period of time, **all** transactions must be recorded in the journal.

Question: How can a balance written down be checked to see if it is correct?

Exercise: *Is the following balance brought forward correct?*

PAGE NUMBER: . . . . . . *02* . . . . . .

Date	Details	Ref.	Received $	Paid $	Balance $
9th May	Balance B/F		15,000	5,000	9,000

Exercise: *Is the following balance brought forward correct?*

PAGE NUMBER: . . . . . . *03* . . . . . .

Date	Details	Ref.	Received $	Paid $	Balance $
30th May	Balance B/F		15,000	9,000	6,000

You might have answered that the above balance is correct. But the balance brought forward cannot be checked just by examining whether the difference between the funds received and those paid out equals the balance. You must compare the entry with the balance made at the bottom of the previous page.

Exercise: *What would the answer to the above question be, if the balance at the bottom of page 02 was as follows?*

PAGE NUMBER: . . . . . . *02* . . . . . .

Date	Details	Ref.	Received $	Paid $	Balance $
30th May	Balance		16,000	8,000	8,000

116

You should view such entries as those above with a great deal of suspicion. For while it is understandable if a mistake is made when transferring the figures forward, for both entries to be different, yet each line to balance is very unlikely to happen unless it was done intentionally.

Exercise: *What reason could the treasurer have in making such entries?*

Hint: What has happened to the $2,000 difference between the two balance entries ($8,000 and $6,000)?

Exercise: *How many of the 11 mistakes can you identify in the following journal entries?*

PAGE NUMBER: . . . .

Date	Details	Ref.	Received $	Paid $	Balance $
30th May	Balance B/F		50,000	20,000	25,000
	Sales of planting materials	08	3,000	———	28,000
3rd May	Purchase of axes		———	2,000	26,000
5th May	Sale of chemicals	08	3,500	———	23,000
6th May	Sale of planting materials	10	2,000	1,000	24,000
30th May	BALANCE		56,500	28,000	24,000

PROJECT DIARY

Question: Will it be useful for the group to keep a project diary?

Question: Who will be the best person to make entries in the diary? Should it be only one person or could any member of the committee make entries?

Question: What information will your group find it useful to record?

Question: Would it be useful to keep a photographic record of the project?

BANK ACCOUNTS

Question: What factors should be considered when choosing the type of bank account the group should have?

Question: How often will the group be making withdrawals from the account?

Question: Who will be the three signatories for the bank account?

Question: How easy will it be for two of the signatories to go to the bank to make withdrawals?

Question: When opening a bank account what information and documents will the signatories require?

Question: When making a withdrawal from a **current account** do the signatories have to go to the bank?

Question: How many signatories are required to sign the group's cheques?

Exercise: *On 1st June, the following bill is received from 'A' Star Supplies Ltd. Write out a cheque for the payment.*

No. *A/003*		BILL		
		"A" STAR SUPPLY Ltd.		
		Affiance, Guyana.		
		Tel: 6433/7856		
Deliver To:				
Name: *Big Development Group*		Date: *29th May 1995*		
Address: *New Community*				
Guyana.				

Quantity	Description	Unit Price $	Value $
2	*1 gallon tins of white paint*	2100	4200
	TOTAL $		4200

118

```
                                              Date:-

THE BANK OF DEVELOPMENT LIMITED.
West Street, Georgetown.

Pay:- .........................................................     ┌──────────────┐
                                                                   │ $            │
     .........................................................     │              │
                                                                   └──────────────┘
     ............................. Dollars.


A/C 3490      No. 20456              --------------------------
```

Exercise: *Identify the three mistakes on the following cheque.*

```
                                              Date:- 31ˢᵗ June

THE BANK OF DEVELOPMENT LIMITED.
West Street, Georgetown.

Pay:- 'A' Star Supply Ltd .................     ┌──────────────┐
                                                │ $4,200.⁰⁰    │
FOUR THOUSAND AND TWO DOLLARS ...               │              │
                                                └──────────────┘
ONLY ──────────── Dollars.


A/C 3490      No. 20456              --------------------------
```

RECORD KEEPING

Question: In addition to financial records, what other documents should a
             group keep secure?

Question: Will the group enter into written contracts?

Question: Will the group receive a loan or grant?
             Will the organization providing the funds require representatives
             of the group to sign an agreement governing the use of the
             funds?

Question: Does the group's secretary keep minutes of the group's meetings?

Question: Is there a list of names of all the group members?

Question: Has the group written or received any letters?

Question: Who should be the person to look after all the group's records and documents?
Should it be just one person?

> **Keep all information safe**

CHAPTER 7
Project supervision

Undertaking a project is similar to going on an adventurous journey. There will be twists and turns and unexpected events. To assist on the journey, maps, tickets and a compass may be needed. Similar aids can be obtained to help a group to manage a project.

The project 'route map' is the ..project plan together with the budget. The procedures used to make a project plan are described in Chapter 3. The plan lists the project activities and the order in which they should be performed. By using the plan, a group will be able to check on the progress of their project. Members can see if activities are being completed at the correct time and in the right order and identify whether delays are occurring.

While the plan is used to confirm that events are happening at the right time, the project budget is employed to check that the project funds are being spent properly. In Chapter 4 the preparation of a project budget and phasing are described. The budget not only states how much money should have been spent and received, but by checking with the planned expenditure phasing, it can be seen whether the project is proceeding according to plan.

Example

In Chapter 4 the example was given of a group of farmers who came together to organize a project which consisted of the following tasks:

- Clearing 50 acres of riverside land.
- Digging a main drainage trench and ditches.
- Planting the land and tending the crops.
- Building a storage bond (a 'lock-up' or secure store).
- Buying and distributing tools and chemicals to the group members.
- Buying a boat and outboard engine.

"PART" PROJECT or ACTIVITIES	EXPENDITURE PHASING				EXPENDITURE TOTAL
	1st Quarter	2nd Quarter	3rd Quarter	4th Quarter	
Land clearance	130,000	200,000	-	-	330,000
Drainage Scheme	100,000	300,000	500,000	-	900,000
Planting crops etc	-	-	20,000	35,000	55,000
Storage Bond	-	10,000	55,000	-	65,000
Tools and Chemicals	-	50,000	55,000	-	105,000
Boat and Engine	400,000	145,000	-	-	545,000
Administration	25,000	25,000	25,000	25,000	100,000
SUB TOTAL	655,000	730,000	655,000	60,000	2,100,000
CONTIN' 15%	98,000	110,000	98,000	9,000	315,000
TOTAL Expenditure	753,000	840,000	753,000	69,000	2,415,000
TOTAL INCOME	-	-	(100,000)	(100,000)	(200,000)
TOTAL FUNDS REQUIRED	753,000	840,000	653,000	(31,000)	2,215,000

121

The planned project budget and phasing was as illustrated on the previous page.

Excluding the amount for contingency, after three months the project expenditure should have been $655,000. In reality it was found to be only $150,000.

A meeting of the group was held and it was found that:

- Land clearance had only just started.
- Because of the delay in commencing the land clearance, work had not started on the drainage scheme.
- The order had not been placed for a boat and engine.
- Administration costs were $65,000 compared to the planned amount of $25,000.

Following discussions, the chairman admitted that he did not have the necessary management skills. The committee had failed to organize the members into working parties to start the land clearance. The administration costs were so high because members of the executive had made a number of unnecessary expenses-paid journeys with overnight stays.

The group members agreed to ask the funding agency to assist them by providing project management training. Following the training, a new management committee was elected.

Monitoring and evaluation

From the above example it can be seen how the project plan and budget can be used to check on project progress. It is important not only to examine the total project expenditure, but also to review the progress and costs of individual project activities.

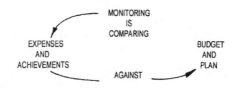

If the achievements (activities) are not in agreement with the project plan, or the expenses with the budget, the following questions should be asked:

- What is the effect?
- Does it matter?
- Is it better or worse?
- What will be the effect on other planned activities?
- What is the overall effect on the project?

It is not necessarily a bad thing when a project does not proceed exactly in accordance with the plan. Equally, it is not necessarily a good thing when a project proceeds exactly in accordance with the plan! During the execution of a project, a group must be prepared to learn and gain experience. Information will become available which will enable the project plan to be reviewed and updated. However, before a project plan is amended, the full effects of the change must be considered.

> A balanced view must be taken
> when evaluating project progress

Decision taking

The success or failure of a project will depend upon the ability of the group to take decisions. It does not matter how good a group is, it will never get all the decisions correct! The important thing is to recognize when a wrong decision has been taken and to take corrective action, and not make things worse by justifying the wrong decision. All decisions have some degree of uncertainty, some more than others. Generally there are two ways of making decisions:

- The **methodical** way. Where all available facts are gathered and analysed, and a prediction of the possible outcomes made before the final decision is taken.
- Using **hunches** or **intuition**. The decision is based on a 'feeling' of what is right, rather than as a result of the analysis of information.

The method individuals use depends upon their training and personality. A good manager knows when to use one method or the other. The methodical method is more suited in a well ordered situation, where all the facts can be collected and examined. However, when uncertainty prevails, it is better to take decisive action quickly. The result of the decision will generate information which will enable a check to be made on whether the correct decision was taken. In other words, in cases of uncertainty, the best thing to do is to do something that will provide information.

> Don't stand there worrying, do something!

When taking decisions, ask, and answer, one question at a time. Try to keep the questions simple. Gather just enough information to enable a decision to be made. If too much information is collected, it will only over-complicate the decision-making process. If the decision is whether to do something, ask:

- **Will it work?**
- **Will the group work it?**

It does not matter how good the committee might consider the decision to be. It will only work if the group members agree and are prepared to put it into practice.

- **Is it worth doing?**
  Some corrective actions cause more problems than the initial problem they are trying to solve.
- **Does it solve the problem?**
  It is pointless doing it unless it works!
- **Can it be seen to make things better, or start to make things better?**
  People will be more prepared to help if they can see that their efforts will be worthwhile.

The advantage of working in a group is that the members usually have a wide range of experience. This should not be ignored, but used for the benefit of the group. If the committee is uncertain what to do, consult and seek advice.

When corrective action has to be taken, do not look at the narrow picture, look at the overall effect on the project.

Examine what are the options; ask:

- What was the cause?
- What is the effect?

When action has to be taken, make a decision and then act decisively. In these circumstances it is very important that once a decision has been taken, all those concerned are informed. Check to make sure that they understand what has to be done.

Conflict resolution

Unfortunately, during a project, not only can activities go wrong, but also conflicts can arise in a group. These should be resolved as soon as possible before they result in permanent damage to the group and disruption to the project. When a disagreement arises, how it will be resolved will depend upon:

- How forceful both sides are.
- How willing they are to work together.

Small misunderstandings and disputes should be resolved as soon as possible. Rather than argue, ask questions and **listen**. If both parties are reasonable an acceptable solution should emerge.

The extreme case is when two factions in a group are both forceful and are not prepared to work together. In these circumstances the assistance of a third party should be sought to mediate between the two groups.

Ultimately, they will have to decide whether they can work together for the

benefit of the whole community or whether the group has to be restructured. The second alternative could have serious implications if external funding is provided in the form of grants or loans. In this case, the funding agency must be consulted immediately.

Managing change

Change is the inevitable result of all projects. Some of the changes will be the desired results of the project while others might be unpredicted consequences. Undesired changes should only happen infrequently in a well managed project. It should be recognized that things are always changing. They only appear to be constant when circumstances and forces which would cause change are balanced by counter forces. As soon as a project begins the process of change is put into place. At the design stage of the project and throughout its execution, the group should be aware of the implications of their activities, and ask:

- How will things change?
- Will things be made better or worse?
- What are the possible desired and undesired consequences of the project activities?

By being sensitive to the consequences of its activities, the group can manage change and control events. Managing is making things happen the way the group wants them to. The group should control events rather than respond to them. To do this the successful project manager must keep informed, plan, monitor, evaluate, make decisions and act. It is not sufficient to be aware of what is happening at the present moment. Plans and predictions should be made on future activities.

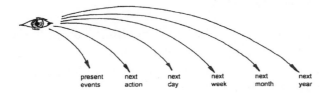

| present | next | next | next | next | next |
| events | action | day | week | month | year |

Good managers know their resources:

- The people they work with.
- The things that have to be used (equipment and materials).
- The available funds (money).

In addition, they are honest with themselves. They recognize their weaknesses and strengths. They compensate for their weaknesses and take advantage of their strengths.

To achieve a successful project result, the group's activities will have to be managed. Management can be provided by members of the executive or committee, or by a specially elected project management committee. It is important that the managers are given the necessary authority and they accept the resulting responsibilities for managing the project.

Managing the project will require working with people. The ideal manager is someone who provides support to the personnel undertaking the project activities. They achieve results through other people working well. Good managers:

- Make sure that the group members who work on the project know what they are expected to do. People are not mind readers! They must be given clear instructions.
- Get everyone to work together in a team.
- Watch that things are being done as required.
- Give advice on how to improve.

To get the group members to work well:

- Give praise.
- Listen and ask for advice and suggestions.
- Give responsibility.
- Treat the group members as individuals.
- Treat everyone fairly.

Managers should not have as their own main objective, proving to others how good they are. Rather, they should strive to help the group members to accomplish the project successfully.

> A good manager achieves results by others working well

Project management

Unlike management of a business, where the employer has authority, management of a group project will rely upon the participants voluntarily giving their full cooperation. This means that the managers will have to be even more sensitive to group members' needs and feelings.

The management style used in dealing with a contractor employed by a group will depend upon the attitude of the contractor. If a contractor is dedicated and honest, very little supervision will be required, other than to ensure that the contractor understands the group's requirements and that agreement is reached on the fees to be paid. When dealing with an unknown contractor, the group's expectations must be made very clear. Also, he must be made to appreciate that the group will only accept work of the required standard for the agreed price. The contractor's activities should be monitored, and any unsatisfactory work brought to his attention. If the contractor fails to respond appropriately to verbal instructions, dated written instructions should be given and a copy kept. Only in extreme cases when the contractor fails to meet the contract requirements should he be dismissed. Problems with contractors can be avoided by the initial careful selection of the contractor. This will be dealt with in more detail in the next chapter.

Financial control

One of the potential sources of conflict in group activities is the use and control of funds. A group's constitution has an important part to play in defining the procedures for the control of expenditure. If a group receives a grant from a funding agency, it will state the required procedures the group has to follow. These will broadly cover procedures for the management of project funds and for record keeping.

To avoid conflict and arguments, before starting the project the group should put in place rules to be followed when the group wishes to spend money. The budget gives details of what the funds should be spent on, and when, but not how or where.

The group should select a number of members to act as a Finance and Purchasing Sub-committee. Its duties would be to:

- Prepare tender documents for contracts; review tenders received for contracts; select contractors to perform work. This will be dealt with in more detail in the next chapter.
- Review quotations for the supply to the group of equipment, materials and services; approve the release of funds to purchase equipment or materials.

The number and membership of the sub-committee should be decided at a meeting of the group members. For practical reasons the committee should consist of at least three members, the approval of any two of whom would be required before funds can be released. There is no hard and fast rule on who the members of the sub-committee should be. They could include members of the executive or committee or other group members. The important thing is that they should be trusted by the group members and experienced in making financial transactions.

It would be impractical to require the sub-committee to approve all expenditure. For example the secretary may need to buy a stamp to post a letter. To cover small expenditures, a petty cash fund could be kept by the treasurer. A limit is set on the maximum amount per item that can be bought from petty cash. Purchases above that limit should require the approval of the sub-committee. When a petty cash account is kept, every item of expenditure must be recorded in a petty cash book used especially for that purpose, and where possible receipts obtained.

Quality control

When working for the group, members might not pay as much attention to quality as they would when performing activities on their own behalf. For this reason attention must be paid to quality control.

- When purchases are made, obtain value for the money spent. Check on the quality and quantity.
- When work is performed, the desired quality must be maintained.

Particular attention must be paid to the quality of work performed by a contractor working for the group. As the project proceeds, quality standards tend to drift and people become more lax in maintaining good standards. For this reason, from time to time standards should be reviewed by the committee.

Planned procurement

For the project to proceed smoothly without unnecessary interruptions, equipment and materials must be made available on time. To achieve this, future events should be examined with the aid of the project plan and a list of the required resources compiled. Many items can be purchased 'off the shelf' and can be readily obtained when required, while others are 'long lead' items, which have to be ordered in advance. Failure to identify long lead items can cause delays.

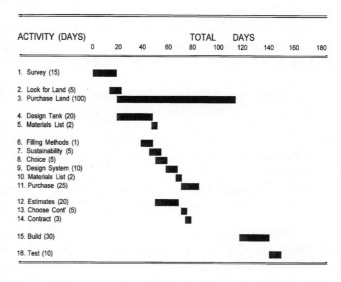

Example

Wood for the construction of buildings should be allowed to season before use. Green (unseasoned) wood shrinks and splits as it dries. Consequently, wood should be purchased in advance of the planned date for starting the construction work.

While it is important to arrange for equipment and materials to be available at the right time, unnecessary purchases should not be made. Money spent at the wrong time is money not available for other use.

Example

In the example of the farming group given at the beginning of the chapter, tools and chemicals are due to be purchased during the second and third quarters. If these were purchased during the first quarter this would result in funds planned for other activities having to be used. This could result in delays in the project if, for example, funds were unavailable to complete the land clearance.

Time management

For the project to be successful, group and committee members will have to devote time to project activities.

Time, like materials, is a resource which has to be managed. If group members have a limited amount of time available to dedicate to the project, then this should be used effectively and not wasted. One way that time is wasted is by keeping people waiting. If a time is set for a meeting or work activity to start, members should make every effort to be there on time. To keep people waiting is to steal their time.

Another form of time wasting is poorly conducted meetings. For example where the chairperson fails to control the meeting, allows discussions to wander off the subject, and the same thing is said over and over again, and still no decisions are made!

Project delays can occur when a few people try to do everything themselves rather than delegate duties to group members. Those selected to manage a group project should appreciate that they have only a limited amount of time available to perform project activities.

> **Time should be used wisely**

Successful project management depends upon the ability to pay attention to detail and to control events rather than to let events dictate what actions must be taken. Good managers are truthful with themselves and know and admit to their own limitations. They are not afraid to look and ask for help. This includes attending training activities.

Questions and exercises

To manage a project successfully, members of the group will require management skills. The following exercises and questions have been devised to enable group members to become familiar with some of the techniques of management.

MONITORING AND EVALUATION

Question: What is a 'bar chart' and how can it be used to plan a project? (See Chapter 3).

Question: What are the key activities of the group's proposed project?

Question: Have the dates when these activities have to be completed been identified?

Question: What would be the overall effect on the project if one or more of the key activities is delayed?

Question: What is meant by the term 'expenditure phasing'? (See Chapter 4).

Question: Will the group require all the project funds at the start of the project?

Question: What is the estimated total expenditure for the first three months of the project?

Question: During the first quarter what activities will require the most funding?

Question: Is it essential that all activities are completed exactly to plan?

Question: How can experience gained while performing project activities be used to modify a plan?

DECISION TAKING

Question: What questions should be taken into consideration before deciding to change a project plan?

Question: What are the two ways that people generally make decisions?

Question: What are the main differences between the two methods?

Question: If all the facts are not available, what can be done to enable decisions to be taken?

Question: During the planning of the project, what was the most difficult decision that had to be taken?

Question: Who took the decision?

Question: How many members of the group were consulted before the decision was taken?

Question: Why is it important to consider the opinions of the group members before making a decision?

Exercise: *It is recognized that a wrong decision has been taken. What should the group do?*

(a) *Ignore the fact and carry on as if nothing has happened.*
(b) *Try to find someone to blame.*
(c) *Decide what corrective action should be taken.*
(d) *Think up a good excuse to try to prove that at the time it was taken it was the correct decision.*

Question: When a problem that could affect a project is discovered, what should be done before deciding upon the corrective action to be taken?

Question: Why is it important to look at the overall effect of the proposed action on the project, before making a decision?

Question: Once a decision has been taken, what action should the committee take next?

Question: What could happen if the group members are not informed of a decision to change the project plan?

CONFLICT RESOLUTION

Question: When members of a group disagree, what are the main factors that control whether they will resolve their differences?

Question: Why might it be better to ask questions and listen to the answers rather than try to persuade persons to change their minds?

Question: If a disagreement occurs in a group, is it better to ignore it in the hope that it might go away or should action be taken to resolve it as soon as possible?

Question: If the conflict in a group gets so bad that it affects the ability of the group to complete a project, what should the group members do?

Question: What role can a funding agency play in resolving group disputes?

MANAGING CHANGE

Question: What changes in the community does the group's project plan to achieve?

Question: What are the possible undesired changes that could occur?

Question: What actions could the group take to ensure that the bad results do not occur?

Question: Do some members of the community oppose the activities of the group?

Question: How can the support of the whole community be obtained?

Question: Is it possible to manage events, or does the group have only limited influence on results?

Question: Is it sufficient just to consider and plan for the next project activity or should a longer term view be taken?

Question: Why is it important that managers should know and understand the resources they will have at their disposal?

Question: What are the group's weaknesses?

Question: How can they be compensated for?

Question: What are the group's strengths?

Question: How can advantage be taken of these strengths?

PROJECT MANAGEMENT

Question: Are there members of the group who have experience in managing projects?

Question: Have members of the group received training in project management?

Question: What is the best way for a group to decide how to manage a project?

Question: Who will manage the group's project?

Exercise: *Review the following two statements and decide which one you agree with:*

(a) If a manager of a project has the objective of proving that he is a good manager, the project is likely to be completed successfully.

(b) If a manager of a project has the objective to assist everyone

who participates to give of their best, then the project is likely to be completed successfully.

What was the reason for your choice?

Question: What steps could group leaders take to encourage the group members to work well and to give of their best for the group?

Question: How is being a group leader different to managing a business that employs staff?

Question: What are the qualities of a good leader?

Question: Is there a difference between being a good leader and a good manager?

Question: What is required for the project to be successful, good leadership or good management?

Question: Is the following statement correct? '*All contractors know what they are doing and should be left to get on with their work without interference from the group*'.

Question: How can a group judge how much a contractor should be supervised?

Exercise: *Which of these statements are correct?*

   (a) A contractor is in business to make as much profit as possible.
   (b) A contractor's first objective is to provide as good a service as possible, so that he will obtain repeat orders.

   (c) To remain in business a contractor has to make a profit, but if he does not provide a good service his reputation will be damaged, and he will soon go out of business.

Question: Why is it important that clear instructions are given to a contractor, stating the group's requirements?

Question: Is it necessary to obtain from a contractor a written estimate of the cost of the planned work?

Question: If a dispute arises between a contractor and a group, why would it be important to have written evidence of agreements made and instructions given to the contractor?

Question: How can a group avoid having problems with a contractor?

Exercise: *Make a list of all the group members who have relevant experience, who can assist and provide advice on supervising a contractor.*

Question: What should be the group's objectives?

(a) To closely control all the contractor's activities.
(b) Assist the contractor to provide a good service to the group.

FINANCIAL CONTROL

Question: Will the group be receiving a grant from a funding agency? Has the agency provided guidelines on its financial control and reporting requirements?

Question: Is it important that rules governing the control of the group's finances are agreed before the work starts on the project?

Question: Has the group agreed on procedures for approving financial expenditure?

Exercise: *Make a list of all the group members who have the trust of all members, and have the relevant experience to manage the group's funds.*

Question: Has the group selected a sub-committee to control the finance and purchasing of equipment and materials?

Question: How many members are there on the sub-committee? Will all the sub-committee's members have to give their approval before money can be spent?

Question: Will the group have a 'petty cash' fund? Who will be responsible for keeping the money safe and maintaining a record of money spent?

Question: What is the maximum amount of money that can be spent from petty cash?

QUALITY CONTROL

Question: Is it necessary to have procedures to ensure that the required quality of work is achieved and maintained?

Question: How can a group ensure that desired standards are maintained?

Exercise: *Make a list of all the group members who can assist in maintaining the standards of material purchased and work done.*

PLANNED PROCUREMENT

Question: What is meant by the terms 'off the shelf' and 'long lead' items?

Question: Has a list been prepared of the equipment and materials that will be required for the group's project?

Question: Are any long lead items required that will need to be ordered well in advance of the time when they will be needed?

Question: Who is responsible for making purchases and placing orders on behalf of the group?

Question: What could be the possible result if, to save time and effort, all the required materials are bought at the same time?

TIME MANAGEMENT

Question: Is time a valuable resource?

Question: Do group members turn up on time for meetings?

Question: Does it matter if meetings start late?

Question: If people are kept waiting for a meeting to start, what else could they be doing at that time?

Question: Are group meetings run efficiently?

Question: What improvements can be made to improve the running of the group meetings?

Question: Do group meetings have agendas and are minutes kept?

Question: How can the delegation of duties save time and improve the efficiency of the group?

Exercise: *Make a list of the qualities of a good project manager.*

Question: Do any group members have these desired qualities?

Question: Will the group require additional training before work commences on the project?

CHAPTER 8
Project execution

As soon as sufficient funds have been obtained, work can commence on the project. What is the first action to be undertaken? And by whom?

Getting started

Before work starts, the group should decide who is going to manage the project. Responsibility can be given to one person or to a project management team. If the project is managed by a team, the duties and responsibilities of each of the team members must be defined. Once this has been done, they must be allowed to manage the project without undue interference. This is not to say they can do what they like and ignore the rest of the group. Regular progress reports should be given to the group committee, and when necessary to all the members of the group.

Preparation of the project plan is described in Chapter 3. The plan, together with the budget, is the route map used to guide and assist the group during the management of the project.

> **When in doubt on what action to take, consult the project plan**

It is likely one of the first actions will be the purchase of materials and equipment. When preparing the project cost estimate, the required resources were identified and listed (see Chapter 4).

Example

The materials list for the construction of a storage bond or secure store could be as shown.

"PART" PROJECT: *CONSTRUCTION OF STORAGE BOND*			
NAME OF SUPPLIER: *ACE SUPPLIES Ltd. Rentown.*			
DESCRIPTION	Quantity	Unit Cost	COST
Soft wood 3" x 3"	*100 BM*	*$30/BM*	*3000*
* ,, 12" x 1"*	*50 BM*	*,,*	*1500*
2" Nails	*2 lbs*	*$20/lb*	*40*
etc.			
		TOTAL	*$ 4540*

When the time comes to place orders, a check should be made that the price estimates previously obtained are still valid. If the prices have greatly increased, then further

136

quotations might have to be obtained from other suppliers. A contingency allowance should have been provided in the budget to cover any increase in costs due to inflation (see Chapter 4).

In the event prices have increased more than the allowance made in the budget, money budgeted for one activity should not be transferred to cover the additional costs of another activity. This could result in all the money being spent before the project is completed. Under these circumstances the group committee must decide whether to amend the project plan, with the possible result that not all the project objectives will be achieved. Or the group can seek extra money to cover the additional costs. If a grant is being provided by a funding agency, the change in circumstances should be reported and their advice sought.

Before purchases are made, the group should ensure that it has a suitable, safe and secure place to store materials.

When orders are placed, the quantity and when appropriate, the quality of the goods to be purchased must be stated. When the goods are received a check must be made to ensure both the quantity and quality are correct. Some products have a limited 'shelf-life' – after a certain date their quality will deteriorate so much that they cannot be used. In some cases it could even be dangerous to use them beyond their shelf-life. Goods should be examined to see if a date is stated on the packaging.

When payment is made for goods, a receipt clearly stating what has been purchased and the amount paid **must** be obtained and kept safe together with any copies of bills and invoices.

> Receipts should be obtained for
> all financial transactions

Employing contractors

If a contractor has to be employed, a costs quotation should be obtained before any agreement is made for doing the work.

To obtain a quotation, the group has to prepare a tender document. This contains a description of the work to be performed together with the terms and conditions controlling the relationship between the group and the contractor. The description of the work could consist of drawings together with written details of the work and specifications. The specifications detail the quality and standards of both the materials to be provided and the work to be performed. To ensure the group will be satisfied with the work, the description should be sufficiently detailed to enable the contractor to know exactly what the group requires. Where possible the group should obtain the help of an expert to assist them in preparing the tender document. Even experts cannot think of everything, so to protect the group from any errors or omissions made in the preparation of the tender document, it is normal to include a 'safety' clause. This clause passes the responsibility to the contractor to ensure, **as far as it is reasonably possible for a competent contractor to do**, that he checks that the description of the works is correct and the work when completed will be fit for the purpose intended.

Example

'It is the responsibility of the Contractor to obtain and become conversant with all information necessary to ensure the complete and satisfactory execution of the Works. The Contractor shall bring to the attention of the Client any errors or omissions in the Tender documents provided to the Contractor.'

To obtain a quotation, the tender documents can be provided to one or more contractors, with a request that they submit their tenders by a given date. Depending on circumstances and custom, contractors might ask for a fee to prepare estimates. If this is the case, agreement should be reached with the contractor that in the event of him being awarded the contract, the amount of the fee paid will be deducted from the total payment for the work.

Example

A contractor required a fee of $10,000 to prepare the estimates for the construction of a road. The fee was paid. The estimated cost was $500,000. On completion of the construction the contractor was paid $490,000, i.e. $500,000 less the $10,000 already paid.

On the 'closing' date for submitting the tenders, those received are examined by the project management team and a selection made. The order should not necessarily be given to the contractor providing the lowest bid. Other factors as well as the price should be considered:

- The quality of the work.
- Whether the work can be completed by the required time.
- If a contractor has previously worked for the group.
- A contractor might offer to do extra work for no additional charge.
- The terms and conditions for payment.

> It is far better and easier to take time in
> selecting a good contractor,
> rather than have the worry and trouble
> of managing a bad contractor

All factors should be taken into consideration before a balanced decision is taken.

Once selection has been made, the group can enter into an agreement with the contractor. A sample agreement for construction works is shown below. A similar format can be used for other types of work.

If a grant is obtained from a funding agency, the agency could require the group to follow its rules and procedures for obtaining tenders and entering into agreements.

FORM OF AGREEMENT

This Agreement made this . . . . . . day of . . . . . . .199 . . .

Between . . . . . .(*enter the name of the Group*) . . . .
in the Country of . . . . . (*enter name of country*) . . . . . .
(hereinafter called the "Client") of the one part
 and . . . . .(*enter the name of the contractor*) . . . . .
in the Country of . . . . . .(*enter the name of country*) . . . . .
(hereinafter called the "Contractor" of the other part Whereas the Client is desirous that certain Works should be undertaken, viz . . . .
. . . . . . (*enter details of the work required. Or if the details are too much for the space available, enter "as per attached schedule"*) . . . . . .
and has accepted the Tender by the Contractor for the construction, completion and maintenance of the Works.

THIS AGREEMENT WITNESSETH AS FOLLOWS:

1. In this Agreement, words and expressions shall have the same meanings as respectively assigned to them in the General and Particular Conditions of Contract hereinafter referred to.

2. The following documents shall be deemed to form and be read and construed as part of this Agreement, viz:
    i)   The said Tender
    ii) The Drawings (if any)
    iii) The Specification (if any)
    iv) The Bills of Quantities and Basic Price List (if any)
    v)   The addenda including Pre contract correspondence (if any)

3. In consideration of the payments to be made by the Client to the Contractor as hereinafter mentioned, the Contractor hereby covenants with the Client to construct, complete and maintain the Works in the conformity in all respects with the provision of the Contract.

4. The Client hereby covenants to pay to the Contractor in consideration of the construction, completion and maintenance of the Works, the Contract Price at the time and in the manner prescribed by the Contract.

5. IN WITNESS WHEREOF the Parties hereto set their hands this . . . . day of . . . . . . 199 . .

    SIGNED FOR AND ON BEHALF OF THE CLIENT   (*signature of the Group representative*)

    IN THE PRESENCE OF   (*signature of witness*)

    SIGNED FOR AND ON BEHALF OF THE CONTRACTOR   (*signature of the Contractors*)

All agreements should state the work to be performed, the total sum to be paid, and also the timing of payments. For a small contract no payments will be made until all the work is satisfactorily completed. However, for larger contracts agreement can be reached with the contractor for fixed percentage payments to be made, throughout the project, on the satisfactory completion of defined activities.

Example

For a contract to build a village hall, the first payment of 10% of the total cost could be made on completion of the foundations. A further 20% could be paid on completion of the walls, and so on.

It is important that the final payment should not be made until the work is completed to the group's satisfaction.

> Do not make the final payment to the contractor until the work has been completed **satisfactorily**

Managing activities

It is likely that members will have to perform project tasks. The way the work is organized will be dictated in part by the project objectives.

Example

A farm project has the objective of increasing the amount of land available for family farms. The initial land clearance could be performed by a contractor using heavy equipment assisted by members working as a group, followed by family groups working on their individual farm plots.

The method used should be selected to ensure the effective control and management of the overall project. The following arrangements could be used.

• Individual members could be employed to do either:

Taskwork. Members would be paid an agreed sum to complete a task. If this method is used, it is important before the work starts that agreement is reached with the person, on exactly what work has to be completed and by when, together with the amount they will be paid. The advantage of this method is that once agreement is reached minimum supervision will have to be provided.

or

Day-work. Members are paid a fixed daily wage. With this system, supervision will have to be provided to instruct the workers on what to do and to check that they are working satisfactorily.

- Small groups can be organized to perform either voluntary or paid work. Depending on the task, these could be either '**family**' or '**neighbourhood**' groups. Similar to taskwork, once the group has been instructed on the work it must do, it can be allowed to organize and manage its own activities, with only minimum supervision being provided by the project management team.

- Large work groups of members can be formed to perform either voluntary or paid work. Like day-work, the project management team will have to provide greater direct supervision.

Irrespective of the method used, responsibility remains with the project management team to ensure the work is completed on time, to the required standard and within the estimated cost.

Throughout the project, the project plan should be used to check that activities are started and completed on time. As discussed in Chapter 3, project activities can be:

- **Independent**, their timing does not depend upon the status of any other project activity.

Example

A craft group receives funds to construct a craft centre and to obtain craft training. The timing of the training does not depend upon the status of the building of the centre.

- **Interdependent**, the timing of activities which are dependent on others, i.e. one activity must be completed before another can begin.

In the above example, the walls of the centre cannot be built until the foundations have been completed!

Some activities can, and in some cases should, be performed at the same time.

Again in the above example, while the foundations are being laid, the materials to build the walls could be purchased.

> Successful project management
> depends on controlling events,
> rather than being controlled by them

141

To avoid delays in the project, future activities should be reviewed to determine what resources will be required, for example, labour, materials, equipment and transportation. Action should be taken to ensure they will be available at the required time.

Project activities must be continuously monitored, information gathered on how the work is progressing, and how project funds are being spent. The facts are used to evaluate the project by assessing to what extent the objectives of the individual activities and those of the project have been accomplished. If the results are not as expected, corrective action might be needed. However, as discussed in Chapter 7, the project plan should not be followed blindly. As the project proceeds, the group members will gain experience which will allow them to review the original plan and judge what amendments, if any, should be made.

Communications and reporting

One of the techniques of good management is communications. Managers cannot make decisions unless they have facts. To do this they must talk with people, to find out what has happened, what is happening and what is likely to happen. If the group's project is being managed by a project management team, they should hold frequent review meetings. In order to inform the group committee of the project status, meetings should be held with them at least once a month.

Writing monthly project reports is a useful management tool. In preparing the report, the management team will have to examine and compare actual activities and expenditure to those planned. In doing this, the project will continuously be monitored and evaluated. A monthly report could contain a brief description of the activities completed during the month and a summary of the project accounts, together with a list of activities planned for the next month. A report is only useful if it is available when required. Those responsible for writing the report should be given a deadline date for completing it, for example, within seven days of the end of the month.

If the group is receiving support from a funding agency, they could have their own reporting procedures that they would want the group to follow. These could include the need to provide detailed statements of expenditure.

Irrespective of the source of funding, the group must keep an accurate record of all money received and spent. In addition to the accounts, proof of all financial transactions must be kept, in the form of receipts, bills and invoices.

If funding is provided by an agency, it is unlikely that all the money will be released to the group at one time. Rather, the funds will be given on completion of agreed activities and after the group has proved that funds already released have been spent in accordance with the project proposal.

Project completion

In Chapter 3 it was suggested that projects are easier to plan if they are organized into smaller 'part' projects. Similarly, the overall management of the project can be assisted by using the completion of these part projects as a measure of the progress of the project. The project management team will have to satisfy itself that a part project has been completed to the required standard and is 'fit for purpose'. To do this, the work will have to be inspected and if necessary tested.

"PART" PROJECT	ESTIMATE OF COSTS					
	LABOUR	MATER'S	EQUIP'	TRANSP'	MISCEL'	TOTAL
Land clearance	100,000	10,000	200,000	20,000	-	330,000
Drainage scheme	575,000	50,000	250,000	25,000	-	900,000
Planting crops etc.	30,000	20,000	-	5,000	-	55,000
Storage bond	20,000	30,000	-	5,000	10,000	65,000
Tools and chemicals	-	50,000	50,000	5,000	-	105,000
Boat and Engine	-	-	500,000	45,000	-	545,000
SUB TOTAL	725,000	160,000	1,000,000	105,000	10,000	2,000,000
ADMINISTRATION @ 5% of estimated project cost						100,000
TOTAL ESTIMATED PROJECT COST						2,100,000

Example

If the part project is the construction of a building, it should be inspected to see that it has been completed in accordance to the plans and specifications. This could involve ensuring that, for example:

During construction:
- *The correct quality materials were used.*
- *The foundations were to the required dimensions and specification.*

On completion:
- *If the walls are painted, that the correct quality and colour of paint and number of coats were applied.*
- *The roof is not leaking!*
- *Any electrical wiring and fittings are installed and are working.*
- *Toilets and water system are working and there are no leaks.*

When is a project finished? A project is undertaken to solve a problem. It is only when that has been accomplished that the project can be regarded as completed. The project management team work on behalf of the group. It is not sufficient for just the team to decide when a project is finished. The final decision rests with the group. When all the part projects have been completed to the satisfaction of the project management team, it must then offer the results of the project for acceptance by the group.

On completion of the project, the project management team should hand over the following to the group:

- A complete and final set of financial accounts, together with all receipts, bills, invoices and bank statements. These should then be audited, checked and verified, by a competent person.

- Copies of all correspondence, minutes of meetings, legal agreements and papers. Operating and maintenance manuals for any equipment.
- An asset inventory, i.e. a list of all buildings, land, equipment, etc. owned by the group.

- Sometimes it is not possible to complete all planned activities in a reasonable time. In these circumstances, rather than wait to complete all the items, the project is offered for acceptance together with a 'punch' list or check-list. The check-list gives a description of all the outstanding actions together with an estimate of any future costs and a date for their completion. Funds for any identified future expenses should be reserved for that purpose.

Example

As part of a project to construct a water distribution system in a village, a water level gauge was to be installed in the reservoir. This had to be purchased from overseas with a delivery time of nine months. The rest of the project activities were completed and the system could work without the gauge. Rather than wait nine months to hand over the project, it was accepted by the community and money set aside for the gauge and its installation.

- A final report on the project. This should include an evaluation of both the project and the lessons learnt in managing the project. Projects are evaluated to determine whether they have achieved the originally set objectives: Where possible, not only the members of the project management team and group committee, but all residents should participate. This would enable all those who are interested to judge and give their views.

During the management of the project, both the project management team and all the group members who participated in the project will gain experience and knowledge. In the future this could be put to the benefit of the community. The participants would provide a great service to the community if they were to share their knowledge and experience with all the residents by organizing a project management review seminar.

> **For the benefit of all,**
> **knowledge and experience should be shared**

> **It's not over yet!**
> **Do not forget the post-project activities**

Questions and exercises

This section will assist the participants to identify the key project management duties.

GETTING STARTED

Question: What are the qualities and experience required to make a good project manager?

Exercise: *List the names of group members who have management experience or are suitably qualified to manage a project.*

Exercise: *List the advantages and disadvantages of the project being managed by:*
(a) One person.
(b) A team of group members.

Question: Should the group's project be managed by just one person or a team?

Question: Should the decision on who is to manage the project be made by the group committee or by all the members at a general meeting?

Question: If it is decided to have a project management team (PMT), is it better for it to be **chosen** by the group committee or **elected** by all the group members?

Question: What is the most important qualification PMT members should possess?
(a) They are popular with the majority of the group members.
(b) They are good managers.

Question: What procedures should be put in place to ensure that the group committee is kept fully informed of project activities?

Question: Will only the group committee be allowed to make all decisions regarding the project or will the PMT have full control?

Question: Should the PMT be allowed to make decisions which could alter the objectives of the project?

Question: Is it possible to agree upon procedures which will allow the PMT to make all the necessary decisions to manage the project?
Can this be done while requiring them to seek the group committee's approval for any action or change in the project plan which might alter the project objectives?

Question: Have the individual members of the PMT been given specific areas of responsibility or will all members be responsible for all activities?

Question: During the planning of the project, were lists prepared of all materials and equipment to be purchased?

Question: Are purchasing activities identified on the project plan?

Question: Has a member of the PMT been appointed to be responsible for making all purchases?

Question: Should decisions on making purchases be based on the initial estimates obtained or should a check on current prices be made before an order is placed?

Question: If all prices have increased since the time the estimates were prepared, how can the group find the additional funds?

Question: When the project budget was prepared, was an allowance made to cover possible increases in prices due to inflation?

Question: In the event that a budgeted contingency allowance is insufficient to cover additional costs, what action should a group take?

Question: Where will the group store materials and equipment purchased? Is it a safe and secure place?

Question: Has the PMT prepared procedures for checking the quality and quantity of all materials and equipment purchased?

Question: What is meant by 'shelf-life'?
            How can it be checked?

Question: Has the PMT agreed on procedures for giving approval for the release of money to pay bills?

Question: Who will make the payments of project costs?

Question: Why is it important to obtain receipts for all payments?

Question: Who will keep the project accounts?

EMPLOYING CONTRACTORS

Question: If a contractor has to be employed, is it necessary to obtain an estimate before an order is placed?

Question: What information should be contained in tender documents?

Exercise: *List the people who can assist the PMT in preparing tender documents.*

Question: If a contractor completes all the work in accordance to the description in the tender document, and it is found not to be 'fit for the purpose', is it the responsibility of the group or the contractor to pay for any corrections?

Question: What are the advantages of asking more than one contractor to provide estimates?
What, if any, are the disadvantages?

Question: If a contractor requires money to prepare an estimate, should the group agree to pay a fee?

Question: Should a contract always be awarded to the contractor giving the lowest cost estimate?

Question: What factors, other than costs, need be considered when deciding who is awarded a contract?

Question: Why is it important to attempt to find out about a contractor before giving him a contract?

Exercise: *Make a list of the people who can assist the group to prepare agreements.*

Question: If the group is receiving a grant from a funding agency, does the agency have procedures that it will want the group to follow when obtaining tenders and entering into agreements?

Question: What information should be contained in an agreement?

Question: Should payments for work by a contractor be paid as one lump sum after the work has been satisfactorily completed, or in stages throughout the work?

MANAGING ACTIVITIES

Exercise: *What types of work are suitable to be performed as day-work and taskwork?*
List the advantages and disadvantages of both systems.

Question: Are any of the group's project activities suitable for taskwork or day-work?
Can they be organized to be done by small or large groups of members?

Exercise: *List the names of all the group members who have the necessary skills and who are prepared to work on project activities.*

Exercise: *Which of these statements is correct?*

(a) Once work is given to groups to perform, the PMT ceases to have responsibility to ensure that it is completed on time, to the required standard and within budget.

(b) It does not matter how the work is organized or who performs it, the PMT is always responsible.

Question: In order to ensure that resources will be available when required, what procedures will the PMT use to review future planned activities?

Question: Why is it important to monitor the progress of a project?

Question: What procedures will the PMT put in place to monitor the progress of the project?

Question: How will the PMT measure that project activities are being completed on time and within budget?

ACTIVITY (DAYS) — TOTAL DAYS
0 20 40 60 80 100 120 140 160 180

1. Survey (15)
2. Look for Land (5)
3. Purchase Land (100)
4. Design Tank (20)
5. Materials List (2)
6. Filling Methods (1)
7. Sustainability (5)
8. Choice (5)
9. Design System (10)
10. Materials List (2)
11. Purchase (25)
12. Estimates (20)
13. Choose Cont' (5)
14. Contract (3)
15. Build (30)
16. Test (10)

Question: Why, during the project, is it not necessarily a bad thing to amend the project plan?

Question: Before a project plan is amended what facts should be taken into consideration?

COMMUNICATIONS AND REPORTING

Question: Will the PMT be required to produce monthly reports?

Question: What information should a monthly report contain?

Question: What is a reasonable deadline to set for completion of a report?

Question: Who will be responsible for keeping the project accounts?

Question: Is it important that all the members of the group committee and PMT are familiar with the accounting procedures to be used?

Question: How frequently will the PMT check the accuracy of the accounts?

PROJECT COMPLETION

Exercise: *Make a list of people who can assist the PMT in inspecting, and if necessary, testing completed 'part projects'.*

Question: Who should decide when a project is completed?
(a) The project management team.
(b) The members of the group committee.
(c) All the members of the group.

Question: Have all the planned activities got to be completed before the project can be 'closed'?

Question: What are 'punch' list or check-list items?

Question: On completion of the project, what information should be provided by the PMT to the group committee?

Exercise: *Make a list of all the people who could perform an audit to check the accuracy of the project accounts.*

Question: On completion of the project, would it be useful for the group to organize a seminar to review the experiences gained during the management of the project?

Exercise: *Make a list of the people who could benefit from attending a post-project seminar.*

> Are there post-project activities to be performed?

CHAPTER 9
Post-project activities

The success of a project can be judged by its sustainability. Will the results of the project continue to benefit the members of the group? In most cases, after the planned activities have been completed there still remains an on-going requirement to sustain the project achievements. A project can only truly be considered concluded when the problem it was organized to solve ceases to exist.

> **For the project to succeed**
> **long-term management might have to be provided**

Post-project management

The group members who were selected to manage the project might not be the ideal ones to provide the necessary on-going supervision. The group will have to decide how it wishes to manage the post-project activities. This could result in a new group committee being elected or a management team being appointed. Or the assets of the group may be handed over to another organization to manage.

Irrespective of the system chosen, those selected must have the necessary management and business skills. Together with all other interested members they can be assisted by organizing training programmes. Assistance can be sought from organizations that can provide advice on running training programmes on management and other commercial and technical subjects.

One of the first post-project activities could be the completion of the final checklist or 'punch list' of items. Once these have been completed, the project accounts can be closed and any remaining funds transferred to the group's general account.

Projects that require further management can be placed into one of two groups:

- Income generating projects, whose activities should make a profit, or at a minimum cover all present and future operating costs.
  Examples of these are: farms, craft groups, small businesses, retail outlets, community centres, community boats.
- Those that will require continued financial support.
  Examples of these are: roads, schools, medical centres, children's feeding programs, mother and baby care.

The management methods employed will depend on the way it is decided to sustain the project objectives.

Example

A project which had the objective of increasing the amount of land being cultivated could be organized as follows:

(a) *The land, cleared and prepared, could be sub-divided into plots and allocated to families to manage. The group would cease to have any further involvement.*

(b) *The land is allocated as (a) above; however, the group collectively organizes the purchase and sale of fertilizers, tools etc. and training programmes on business and agricultural topics.*

(c) *As (b) above, but the group has the additional task of managing the marketing of the products of the individual family farms. A fixed percentage of the sales is retained as a fee for providing the marketing service.*

(d) *The land and facilities are entirely managed by the group with members employed to work on the community farm.*

In the case of (a) above, the individual families are entirely responsible for managing their own farms, without assistance. The other extreme is detailed in (d) above, where the group retains full control of all activities. All the cases have one thing in common, if the farms are to prosper they must make enough money to cover all costs.

Management of profit making enterprises

Whether the operations are performed collectively or by a number of smaller groups, the same business principles apply. It is beyond the scope of this book to cover in detail the organization and management of income generating operations. Suitable books can be obtained on small business management, enterprise development and organizing co-operatives.[1]

However, briefly: If the group is going to manage an income generating business, it will have to earn sufficient money to meet current operating costs, funds to cover future planned and unplanned expenditure, and profits to be used for the benefit of group members.

During the project stage a plan and budget was used as a management guide. Similarly, operating plans and budgets should be used as aids to business management.

The objective of the business must be agreed on and a mission statement prepared. This statement summarizes the goals to be achieved.

---

[1] One such book is *Improve Your Business*, edited by D.E.N. Dickson, published by International Labour Organisation, 1986

Example

The mission statement of a community boat could be:
'The boat shall be used to provide a safe, regular and economical service to all community members. Fares charged shall be calculated to provide funds to cover operating costs and provision made to purchase, when required, a replacement boat. Any surplus funds shall be used to fund the running of the community centre.'

Once the mission statement is agreed on, an operating plan can be prepared. Planning is thinking out in detail what the intended business activities are and how they are going to be performed.

A business plan is the estimate of future sales, costs and profit which are thought achievable.

In preparing the plan, questions to be answered are:

- What shall we sell?
- How much do we want to sell?
- How will we do it?
- How long will it take?

Except for persons running a shop these questions look to be inappropriate. A farmer may feel that more suitable questions would be:

- What shall I grow?
- How shall I grow it?

However, it does not matter whether the business is farming, manufacturing or providing a service, the important thing is that it will only make money when the product or service is sold. Therefore, when preparing a plan, an estimate must be made of the potential sales. If the market is large, then the controlling factor will be the capacity of the business, i.e. the size of the farm, the number of craft workers, etc. However, if the market is limited, it would be pointless to produce products that could not be sold.

A sales estimate for the following twelve months should be prepared. To do this an estimate has to be made, for each month, of:

- The level of business, i.e. how much is going to be made/grown and sold, or services provided.
- The prices charged.
- The total sales, which equals price multiplied by the number sold.

Example

The sales estimate for the first six months of operation of a chicken farm could be as follows:

152

Number of chickens sold	20	15	30	20	30	20
Price (each)	500	500	500	500	500	500
Sales per month	10,000	7,500	15,000	10,000	15,000	10,000

The estimates are based on the sale of chickens at an average weight of 5 lb at a price of $100 per lb.

An estimate should be prepared of the operating costs for the following twelve months. This should include all the expected costs.

For the above example, the costs per month could be as illustrated, based on: the purchase of 35 day-old chicks per month at a cost of $100 each. Feeding 60 birds, 2 lb each at a cost of $30 per lb. The farmer pays himself $1,000 per week.

Details		Cost per month $
Purchase of day old chicks		3500
Feed		3600
Drugs		300
Labour:	Hired	-
	Self	4000
	Family	-
Transportation		500
Other		-
TOTAL COST PER MONTH		11,900

After the Sales and Costs estimates have been prepared, they can be used to determine whether the business will be profitable.

For the first six months of the operation of the chicken farm the profit/loss estimate would be:

Sales	10,000	7,500	15,000	10,000	15,000	10,000
Costs	11,900	11,900	11,900	11,900	11,900	11,900
Profit	–	–	3,100	–	3,100	–
Loss	1,900	4,400	–	1,900	–	1,900

For the first six months the estimated total surplus is $6,200 with a loss of $10,100. This is an estimated net loss of $3,900. If this continues the farmer will soon go out of business!

153

The profit/loss estimates will indicate whether the business will achieve its objectives.

> **The objective of a business should be to make a profit**

Profits can be increased by increasing SALES while decreasing COSTS.

Sales depend on the **price** of the product and the amount sold. Costs depend on the **cost** of producing the product.

Costing: Is the **calculation** of how much each item costs to produce or how much it costs to provide each service. This is done by listing all the things money will be spent on in running the business and estimating how much each one will cost.

Costs should be examined to see if any money can be saved, by paying less or doing it another way.

Pricing: Is the way of **deciding** how much to charge for each product or service.

Normally the price received is controlled by market forces:

- The **supply**: the amount available for sale.
- The **demand**: how many customers there are.
- What **competitors** are charging for a similar product.

Calculating the cost of a product is relatively uncomplicated. However, fixing the price is far more difficult as there are a number of factors influencing how much people are prepared to pay for a product or service. It will take some time for those running a new business to get to know the market. Running a business is not just producing the product or providing the service. Equally important is the marketing of the product or service. Marketing is getting people to want the goods and services, selling them, delivering them and getting paid for them.

Successful marketing is achieved by working hard to increase sales. This can be done by:

- Finding out what the customers want.
- Providing the product or service that satisfies those wants.
- Setting the right price.
- Advertising and promoting the product.

Advertising is telling people what the group has to sell so that they will want to buy those products rather than those of the group's competitors. Promotion includes every way the group can influence people to buy their product.

Every effort should be made to promote a good image of both the business and the product. Customers should be encouraged to think 'it's the **BEST**'. By keeping a check on the quality, the group should try to ensure that it is 'the **BEST**'.

The importance of keeping records during the management of the project was stressed in Chapter 8. Likewise, when running a business, plans and estimates have to be made, activities have to be monitored and evaluated and decisions taken. To do this effectively, requires information. Keeping records provides information.

- Keep a copy of all letters sent and received.
- Keep a journal to record all money received and spent.
- Keep all bills, invoices and receipts.
- Keep a record of all wages paid.
- If goods or services are provided on credit, keep a record of how much money customers owe.
- Keep a business diary, to write down the main things that happen in the business.

Example

For a farm operation, this could include what, when and how much of each crop was planted and harvested. For a manufacturing activity, you would record what, when and how things were made. If services such as a community boat are provided, make a note of how many trips were made, where to, how many passengers there were, how much fuel was used, and so on.

Do not throw information away, keep it: one day it might be important

If a group participates in the management of a profit making enterprise, consideration should be given to the distribution of profits.

Example

In the land cultivation project described on p. 151, in one case each family is responsible for the management of its own farm plots and none of the profits made go to the group. However, in the other cases the group participates in the management of profit making operations. There are several ways in which the group profits could be used, including:

- *Each year the profits could be distributed equally to each of the group members.*
- *The profits could be shared to each family in proportion to the total amount of fertilizer, etc, purchased during the period.*
- *Any profits made can be used to finance other group or community activities, for example, start other projects, help fund the community's school or health service etc.*

To avoid any disagreements, once the group has agreed on the method of distribution of profits, the procedures should be stated in the group's constitution.

> **If the group's activities make a profit,
> the way it will be distributed
> should be stated in the group's constitution**

Management of non-profit making group activities

If the group has to manage a **non-income generating** venture, it has to consider whether it would be more effective for the group to hand over the assets of the project to another organization to manage. In some cases, for practical reasons, the group might have been originally established only to manage the project phase, with the intention of allowing the government or local council to have the long-term responsibility for operations.

Example

The rules of a number of funding agencies specifically prohibit grants to be provided to government organizations. In these cases, an independent non-government organization (NGO) can be formed to obtain funds to build a school or some other community amenity. Once it is constructed, it is handed to the local council or government ministry to manage.

If, however, the group wishes to continue to be responsible for the management of the post-project activities, it has to consider and decide upon operating objectives. In doing this, one of the most important considerations is sustainability, the ability of the project to continue to function for as long as required.

> **Unless a project can continue to fulfil its objectives
> for as long as it is required,
> it can be considered to have failed**

Similar to managing a business, an operating plan and budget should be prepared as a management aid. Given the operating objectives, the operating plan and budget can be devised.

Example

Funds were provided to a group to construct communal toilets. After construction, the community members selected a group of residents to manage the facilities. The objectives were decided to be to maintain clean, well repaired public toilets.

The following operating plan was formulated:

(a) A cleaner would be employed to clean the facilities once a week.
(b) It was estimated that the cesspit would have to be emptied twice a year.
(c) Minor repairs would be required every year, and the building painted every two years.

An operating budget was then prepared:

	$
Cost of cleaning	
Labour at $100 per week	5,200
Cleaning materials at $50 per week	2,600
Emptying of cesspit, $5,000 each time	10,000
Minor repairs	1,000
Provision for painting $5,000 per year	5,000
Total annual operating cost	23,800

For a business, estimates of sales have to be made. However for non-income earning activities the group will have to organize fund-raising. Applications can be made to funding agencies for a grant to cover operating costs, or the group can organize their own fund-raising activities.

In the above example, the group decided to raise their own funds to cover the $23,800 annual cost. Two schemes were considered:

(a) A number of fun days could be organized, and the profits used to cover the operating costs.
(b) A collection of $10 per week would be made from the 50 houses in the community.

Due to the possible problems of making collections, the first option was chosen and three fun days were run, making a total profit of $29,500.

If the group's operations require financing, an accurate record of all money received and spent, whether from grants or self help activities, must be kept.

Even though the group is not running a profit-making business, plans and estimates have to be made, activities have to be monitored and evaluated and decisions taken. To do this effectively requires information. Keeping records provides information.

- Keep a journal to record all money received and spent.
- Keep all bills, invoices and receipts.
- Keep a record of all wages paid.

- Keep a group activities diary, to write down the main things that happen.
- Keep a copy of all letters sent and received.

Whether profit making or not, one of the reasons that projects fail is that the facilities are not looked after or maintained.

Examples

Roads constructed by groups are not repaired, and soon deteriorate. Pumps installed in community water supply systems are not maintained, parts are stolen and damaged pipes not repaired. Community Centres are allowed to fall into disrepair, repairs and redecoration are not done. Chainsaws and farm equipment are misused and not serviced.

If machinery and equipment are purchased as part of the project, the group should ensure that they are correctly operated and maintained. Similarly, if the group owns buildings, they should be regularly inspected and when necessary, repaired and redecorated. Group members should be selected to be responsible for the facilities and, if necessary, trained to perform their duties.

> **Group members should be selected to be responsible for looking after group facilities**

Even equipment which is correctly operated and well maintained cannot last forever. At some time it will have to be replaced. This will require money. If a project is to be self sustaining, funds must be set aside from income to be used to buy replacements or pay for repairs.

> **Provision should be made to cover future replacement costs**

Managing a non profit making undertaking can be more difficult than running a business. With time, the enthusiasm of the group members might decline and people will be less prepared to devote time to group activities. Members may fail to turn up for meetings. If the original objectives still have to be accomplished, the committee will have to encourage the members to continue to take an active interest in the group's activities. This can be done by demonstrating to members the possible resulting disadvantages if the group was to cease to function.

In the life of all groups the time will come when the members must decide whether the group has a continued useful function to fulfil or whether it should be disbanded. No group should continue just for its own sake. When the group ceases to perform a useful function, it should disband, with the members delighted, knowing that the group has achieved its objectives.

Project accomplished

Questions and exercises

All the group's efforts will be wasted unless arrangements are made to maintain and manage the project for as long as it is required by those who benefit from its results.

Management procedures will have to be tailored to meet the present and future objectives of the group members. Questions and exercises for both profit and non-profit activities are included in this section.

Question: What problem was the group's project organized to solve?

Question: What (if any) are the long term objectives of the project?

POST-PROJECT MANAGEMENT

Question: Are there other organizations which could manage the post-project activities for the group?

Exercise: *List the advantages and disadvantages of the remaining activities being managed by:*
(a) The group.
(b) Other organizations.

Exercise: *Make a list of the relevant experience and qualifications the members of the group committee should have to manage the post-project activities.*

Question: Do the members of the current group committee have the required qualifications and experience?

Question: When the project phase has been completed, should group members be given the opportunity of selecting a new committee?

Question: What training will the committee require to assist it to manage the group's affairs?

Question: Are there members of the community or external organizations who could provide the training?

Question: What (if any) project 'check-list' items remain to be completed?

Question: Have funds been allocated to complete the work?

Question: Who has been made responsible for organizing the work?

MANAGEMENT OF PROFIT MAKING ENTERPRISES

Question: Will the group be required to manage all the activities, or will some be managed by individuals or family groups?

160

Question:	Has agreement been reached on the allocation of management responsibilities?
Question:	Where can the group get more information and advice on running a business?
Question:	What are the objectives of the group's business?
Exercise:	*Devise a mission statement for the group's business.*
Question:	Is it necessary for every business to have an operating plan?
Question:	What is the product or (service) the group is going to sell?
Question:	How much is planned to be sold?
Question:	What factors should be taken into account when determining the price of a product?
Question:	Where will the group sell its product?
Question:	Will sales be made throughout the year or only at specific times?
Question:	Who (if any) are the group's main business competitors?
Question:	What do they charge for their products?
Question:	Do they advertise their products or services?
Question:	Why do customers buy from them rather than any other business?
Question:	What price will the group charge for each product (or service)?
Exercise:	*Make an estimate, for the next twelve months of operations, of the total sales per month.*
Question:	What will be the total value of sales for the year?
Question:	How will the group obtain the product (or provide the service)?
Question:	What resources (labour, equipment, materials, energy, transportation) will be required ?
Question:	Will the group have to employ staff?
Question:	How much will they be paid?
Question:	What equipment will be required?
Question:	What will be the operating cost of the equipment?

Question: Who will operate the equipment?

Question: Who will maintain the equipment?

Question: What materials will have to be purchased?

Question: Who can supply the materials?

Question: How much will the materials cost?

Question: Will the group have to pay electricity bills, purchase gasoline or other fuel?

Question: Will the group have to hire transportation to collect material, or to deliver its goods?

Exercise: *Estimate the operating cost for the business for one year.*

Question: What is the estimated total operating costs for next year?

Question: Will the group's business make an estimated profit or loss next year?

Question: Will enough profit be made to set some money aside to cover the future costs of purchasing replacement equipment?

Question: What steps could be taken to increase the profits?

Question: Can savings be made in the costs?

Question: Can increased sales be achieved?

Question: Can more products be sold?

Question: Can higher prices be obtained?

Question: What factors control the prices that can be obtained?

Question: What can the group do to get more customers?

Question: Have rules been agreed on how profits should be shared or used?

Question: Does the group have a constitution?

Question: Are the rules for profit distribution stated in the constitution?

MANAGEMENT OF NON-PROFIT MAKING GROUP ACTIVITIES

Question: Is there another more suitable organization to manage the activities?

Question: Are the group members willing to hand over the responsibility to another organization?

Question: Is the other organization willing to accept the responsibility?

Question: What do the group members consider to be the ongoing operating objectives?

Question: What steps will the group have to take to safeguard the future of the project?

Exercise: *Make a list of all the activities required to ensure sustainability. Identify those activities that will require funding.*

Question: What resources (labour, materials, transportation, etc) will have to be provided to achieve the operating objectives?

Question: Will the labour requirement be provided by voluntary or paid activity?

Question: Who will be responsible for organizing the activities?

Question: Will materials have to be purchased?

Exercise: *Make an estimate of one year's operating costs.*

Question: How will the group fund the operating costs?

Question: Can financial assistance be provided by a grant from an aid agency?

Question: Will the group be able to obtain all or part of the funds by self help?

Question: What activities or methods can the group use to obtain the necessary funds?

Question: Why is it important to keep records?

Question: Who will be responsible for keeping the group's financial records?

Exercise: *List the advantages and disadvantages of keeping a business and group activities diary.*

Question: Does the group own any equipment or buildings?

Question: Who is responsible for their safekeeping?

Question: Who is responsible for their maintenance?

Question: Is the use of group equipment restricted to only a few members or can anyone use them?

Exercise: *List the advantages and disadvantages of having restricted and unrestricted use of equipment.*

Question: Have those members responsible for the maintenance and operation of equipment received any training?

Question: Does the group have maintenance and operating manuals for their equipment?
Who is responsible for keeping them?

Exercise: *Estimate the expected operating life of each of the items of group equipment.*
At the end of their useful life will replacements have to be bought?

Exercise: *If an item of equipment costs $100,000 and it has an estimated useful life of 10 years, how much money should be set aside each year to cover the replacement cost?*

Question: How often should the group's buildings be inspected?

Question: How often should the group's buildings be painted?

Question: Who is responsible for inspection and maintenance of buildings?

Question: Should a group remain in existence, even if only the committee takes any interest in its activities?

Question: What factors should be taken into account when considering whether a group should continue or cease to function?

Question: Has the group achieved all its objectives?

Question: If objectives are still to be achieved, what action can the committee take to maintain the active support of the members?

Question: Should a group disband when all it can accomplish has been achieved?

> ### Congratulations
> ### on accomplishing the group's objectives!